The 2008 Elections in Florida

Change! But Only at the Top of the Ticket

Robert E. Crew, Jr. and Slater Bayliss
with the assistance of Monica L. Moore

Patterns and Trends in Florida Elections Series

UNIVERSITY PRESS OF AMERICA,® INC.
Lanham • Boulder • New York • Toronto • Plymouth, UK

University Press of America,® Inc.
4501 Forbes Boulevard
Suite 200
Lanham, Maryland 20706
UPA Acquisitions Department (301) 459-3366

Estover Road
Plymouth PL6 7PY
United Kingdom

British Library Cataloging in Publication Information Available

Library of Congress Control Number: 2010942483
ISBN: 978-0-7618-5426-5 (paperback : alk. paper)
eISBN: 978-0-7618-5427-2

For Catherine Anne Crew,
Sara Brooks and Blair Bayliss

Contents

List of Illustrations vii

Preface ix

Part I The 2008 Presidential Election in Florida

1 An Overview 3
- Introduction 3
- The 2008 Election in Historical Perspective 4

2 The Florida Presidential Primaries 5
- Introduction 5
- Who Were the Candidates? 6
- How the Florida Primaries Were Contested 7
- Summary 13

3 The General Election in Florida 15
- The Strategic Context 15
- Positioning, Targeting and Message 16
- How the Democrats Campaigned: The Ground Game 17
- How the Democrats Campaigned: The Air Wars 21
- How the Republicans Campaigned: The Ground Game 23
- How the Republicans Campaigned: The Air Wars 25

4 The Election Results 27
- Early and Absentee Voting 28
- The Pattern of Results 32
- The County-by-County Results 34
- Explaining Increased Competitiveness 36

Part II Voting Behavior in the Florida Presidential Election

5 Who Voted and in What Numbers? 43
- Voter Registration and Turnout in Florida in Historical Perspective 44
- Voter Registration in the 2008 Election 44
- Voter Turnout in the 2008 Election 51
- Turnout across Counties 51

6 Social Groups and the Vote 56
- Group Voting in Florida: 2004 and 2008 56
- Group Voting: Florida and the Nation 62
- Summary 65

7 Candidates and Issues in the 2008 Campaign 66
- The Concerns of the Electorate 66
- Candidate Qualities 70

Part III The Congressional Elections

8 The Outcome of the 2008 Congressional Races 75
- Introduction 75
- District by District Analysis 78
- Incumbency Success 94
- Explaining Incumbency Success: Challenger Quality and Campaign Spending 96
- Summary 106

Part IV The State Legislative Races

9 The Outcome of the 2008 Election Cycle 109
- Introduction 109
- Outcome 111
- Explaining Non-Competitiveness: The Cocktail of Apportionment, Incumbency, and Term Limits 112
- The Effects of the Cocktail in the 2008 Legislative Campaigns 114
- Minor Party Candidates 116
- Tight Legislative Races 117

Part V The Florida Elections of 2008 in Perspective

10 The 2008 Elections and the Future of Florida Politics 125
- State Legislative Elections 126
- Legislative Reapportionment 127

Bibliography 129

Index 133

Illustrations

FIGURES

2.1. The Battle for the Republican Nomination in Florida 10

4.1. The Battle for Florida 28

4.2. Presidential Voting Trends in Florida, 1998–2008 35

TABLES

4.1. Distribution of Early, Absentee, and Election Day Voting 30–31

4.2. Presidential Vote Outcomes in Florida (1960–2008) 33

4.3. Distribution of Vote by County (2004–2008) 37–39

5.1. Voter Registration in Florida and the Nation (1968–2008) 45

5.2. Voter Registration in Florida by Party Affiliation (1972–2008) 46

5.3. Voter Registration in Florida by County (2004–2008) 48–49

5.4. Voter Turnout in Florida by County (2004–2008) 52–54

6.1. Social Groups and the Presidential Vote in Florida (2004–2008) 58–59

6.2. Social Group Voting in Florida and the Nation 2008 63–64

7.1. Most Important Problems as Seen by Electorate in Florida and the Nation 67

7.2. Concern about the Economy 68

7.3. Concern about the War in Iraq 68

7.4. Concern about the Race of the Candidates in Florida and the Nation 71

7.5. Concern about Negative Ads 72

8.1. Distribution of Congressional Seats in Florida, by Party (1952–2006) 76–77

8.2. Incumbency Electoral Success, Florida and the Nation (1982–2008) 94

8.3. Competitiveness in Florida Congressional Elections (1982–2008) 95

8.4. Campaign Funds of Florida Congressional Candidates in 2008 97–99

8.5. Congressional Candidates Background and Experience, Competitive Races 100–101

8.6. Congressional Candidates Background and Experience, Non-Competitive Races 102–105

9.1. Distribution of Legislative Seats in Florida by Political Party (1980–2006) 110

Preface

As Florida has become politically more competitive, it has become more important in American national politics and in presidential elections. With the possibility that its electoral vote can be cast for either of the national political parties, and that this vote can be critical to their national success, both the Democrats and the Republicans have been pushed to contest the presidential election in the state at very high levels of effort.

The Florida elections of 2008 were widely anticipated. In the aftermath of the disputed contest in 2000, both the Republicans and the Democrats had re-doubled their efforts to organize and motivate their supporters and the Republicans in particular saw the state as crucial to their chances of winning the presidency. Concurrently, demographic changes were taking place that threatened to alter voting behavior in both U.S. Congressional and Florida State Legislative races. In the aftermath of the election, political partisans as well as more objective observers sought to explain the outcome, to understand the extent to which the state had shifted its overall partisan alignment and to divine the direction that the voters were likely to take in the near future.

This book speaks to questions about each of these topics. It was stimulated by queries from students and from discussions with our friends who are active participants in electoral politics in Florida. The book also drew inspiration from the work of Paul Abramson, John Aldrich and David Rohde who for over 30 years have described and analyzed the outcomes of American national elections and thereby contributed immeasurably to our understanding of voter participation, electoral choice and the changing nature of American political parties. We hope to make similar contributions to the study of Florida political parties and elections.

The analysis relies on a wide variety of evidence. The examination of the nomination process is based on interviews with participants from both the major political parties in Florida and from the individual campaigns as well as on news coverage of these campaigns. Data about the results of the election—voter registration, vote totals, voter turnout—came from the Florida Department of State, Elections Division. TNS Media Intelligence provided data on television expenditures and polling data came from MSMBC Exit Polls.

This is the first of what we expect will be a continuing series of books on elections in Florida. It will be followed by a similar analysis of the 2010 Gubernatorial and other statewide offices, Senatorial, Congressional, and State Legislative elections. The state is large and diverse and warrants examination as something of a political guide on for political action throughout the nation. But the state also deserves attention in its own right, as a fascinating example of electoral behavior in a unique political system. Floridians need to know more about how their elected officials come to represent them.

The inclusion of Monica Moore's name on the book cover indicates her importance to our effort. Without her assistance in gathering and organizing the data upon which the analysis was based, the book simply could not have been completed. As she goes off to graduate school at the University of North Carolina, we wish her well. We would also like to acknowledge the help of Professor Brad Gomez of the Florida State University Political Science Department whose careful reading and insightful comments about the book improved it considerably. And finally we would like to thank several active members of both the Democratic and Republican Parties in Florida who provided us information for the book and also helped clarify our analysis.

Part I

THE 2008 PRESIDENTIAL ELECTION IN FLORIDA

Chapter One

An Overview

INTRODUCTION

Elections are pivotal events in democracies. They confer power on individuals and on political parties and provide the electorate a mechanism through which it can indicate preferences on issues of public policy.

Over time elections reveal patterns and trends in public attitudes, in political interest and in levels of support for candidates and parties. Understanding these tendencies equip the polity to nurture and refine its system of government. This book seeks appreciation of these electoral patterns in the State of Florida.

Understanding presidential elections and politics in an individual state is important in its own right since presidential elections are not national elections. Rather, they are individual state elections aggregated to the national level and national outcomes over time can be substantially affected by the changes in voting behavior at the state level.

Presidential elections may be especially important in Florida, which is the fourth largest state in the nation and often seen as a bell weather for political activity throughout the nation. If, as occurred in 2008, the Florida electorate changes its behavior, the national outcome can be altered. Thus we seek answers to several questions in Florida that may have implications for national politics. These include, obviously, which political party was successful? How did the candidates campaign? Who, that is which social groups, voted? How did these groups vote? What issues and attitudes motivated the electorate? How did voters evaluate the performance of candidates and political parties? What were the partisan preferences and loyalties of the electorate? And how much money was raised and spent in the elections? In an effort to put Florida into the context of the national election, answers to these questions in the state are compared to the answers to identical questions at the national level. The answers are also placed in the context of previous elections in the state.

THE 2008 ELECTION IN HISTORICAL PERSPECTIVE

In the lexicon of *The American Voter*, (Campbell, Converse, Miller and Stokes. 1961) the presidential election of 2008 in Florida, and in the nation, can be defined as a "reinstating election," one in which the party with the "normal vote" advantage was returned to office after being displaced by "short term factors" in previous years. However, in contrast to the national outcome, the vast majority of Congressional and state legislative seats in Florida, which have been in the hands of the Republicans for over a decade, were maintained by that party. In this book we explore the reasons for these disparate outcomes.

Throughout the history of Florida, the Democratic Party has been the majority party, whether majority was defined with survey data or with voter registration figures. Nevertheless, between 1980 and 2008, Democratic presidential candidates were the victors only in 1996 and in 2008. In the remaining years, a variety of important issues and the differential appeal of the candidates involved pushed Democratic voters to cast their ballots for Republican candidates in a series of "deviating elections." At the same time, many Floridians, as was the case with citizens throughout the nation, retreated from identification with any political party and a period of partisan de-alignment began. Thus, particularly after 1988, presidential elections in Florida were close, but the Republicans almost always won. A majority of the electorate did not, however, shift its psychological loyalty to the Republicans and that Party never had an edge in partisan attachment (party ID) over the time period, nor did it have a majority in voter registration. That is, the Florida electorate never "realigned," and in the presidential election of 2008 it came back home by casting a majority of votes for Barack Obama. Much of the analysis in this book is devoted to an explanation of this phenomenon.

Chapter Two

The Florida Presidential Primaries

INTRODUCTION

Florida is the fourth largest state in the nation, has 27 electoral votes and sends large delegations to both the Republican and the Democratic Party nominating conventions. In 2008 the Democrats had 211 delegates and the Republicans had 114. These numbers are highly prized and should be the focus of great attention. Traditionally, however, the date for the primary has been mid-March, well after the Iowa caucuses, the New Hampshire and South Carolina primaries and "Super Tuesday" and the time when, in many years, the outcome of the race had already been decided. Thus Floridians have been frustrated by their lack of influence on the candidate selection process and, not incidentally, by the relatively paltry amount of money spent on presidential campaigns in the state in comparison to the amount contributed to these campaigns.

In 2007 the Florida legislature made a dramatic attempt to address this problem by voting to move the primary to January 29, hoping that candidates would be forced to spend more money in the state and would be pushed to address issues of concern to the Florida electorate. Unfortunately, this action violated national party rules and both major parties responded with sanctions; the Republicans cut the Florida delegation in half, but the Democrats disenfranchised *all* their delegates. In solidarity with the national party, the Democratic presidential candidates also pledged to boycott the primary altogether. These actions had implications for both parties, perhaps more important for the Democrats.

WHO WERE THE CANDIDATES?

The Republican Primary

When Vice President Dick Cheney chose not to seek the nomination, the race for the Republican presidential nomination became the first such primary since 1928 in which neither an incumbent President nor a former Vice President sought the party's nomination, and a variety of candidates, some more serious than others, announced their intentions to run. At the beginning of 2007, these included John H. Cox, a long time unsuccessful candidate for office in Illinois, Senator Sam Brownback of Kansas, former Governor of Virginia Jim Gilmore, and former Governor of Wisconsin and U.S. Cabinet member Tommy Thompson. In early January, former Governor of Massachusetts Mitt Romney announced that he was forming an exploratory committee. Subsequently, others came into the field, including U.S. Congressman Ron Paul, former Arkansas Governor Mike Huckabee, Rudy Giuliani, former Mayor of New York City, U.S. Senator John McCain, U.S. Congressman Duncan Hunter and U.S. Congressman Tom Tancredo. Alan Keyes and former Senator and actor Fred Thompson entered the race later in September. Five of these candidates, Gilmore, Thompson, Brownback, Tancredo and Cox dropped out of the race before the Iowa caucuses. Only Huckabee, Giuliani, Romney, and McCain mounted serious campaigns in Florida, but the state served as a pivotal event in the ultimate outcome of the Republican nomination race.

The Democratic Primary

With George Bush's second term coming to an end and with no Republican Vice President on the ticket, the presidency became an "open" seat, one that Democrats thought they had a real chance at winning. Thus vigorous activity in the Democratic presidential primary began in the aftermath of the 2006 Congressional elections. Between November 2006 and February 2007, eight serious candidates opened campaigns for the nomination: U.S. Senators Joe Biden, Hillary Clinton, Barack Obama and Chris Dodd, former Senator and 2004 vice presidential candidate John Edwards, Bill Richardson, Governor of New Mexico, former Governor of Iowa Tom Vilsack, and Congressman Dennis Kucinich. Former Alaska Senator Mike Gravel announced his candidacy in April 2006.

In the first three months of 2007, three of these candidates raised serious money, separated themselves from the remainder of the field and remained the frontrunners throughout the campaign. Both Hillary Clinton and Barack Obama raised more than $20 million each and John Edwards raised more than $12 million.

As the primary season began and Florida moved the date of its primary from mid March to January 29, the Democratic National Committee ruled that the Florida delegates to the Democratic National Convention would not be seated or, if seated, they would not be able to vote. In response, the presidential candidates signed a pledge not to campaign in Florida, even though their names were already on the ballot, and for the most part, kept their promises.

HOW THE FLORIDA PRIMARIES WERE CONTESTED

The Republicans

National tracking polls beginning January 18, 2007 showed Rudy Giuliani leading the Republican field in the nation at large, with John McCain second and Mitt Romney third. Beginning in May of that year, Romney began to close the gap on McCain and by June 12, had pulled into second place. From that point until December 3, with two exceptions in September of 2007, McCain consistently ran third behind Guiliani and Romney and beginning in September, when Mike Huckabee began to emerge as a serious candidate, usually ran fourth. (Rasmussen Report. *Weekly Presidential Tracking Poll History*. Www.rasmussenreports.com. Retrieved 2/23/2009)

At the national level, all the candidates except Giuliani adopted the traditional nominating strategy of contesting the early primaries and caucuses in an effort to show strength and build momentum. Giuliani decided to forego this strategy and to "turn upside down the laws of political gravity" by targeting Florida as the place to initiate his campaign. He hypothesized that the campaign really began on Jan. 29 in Florida and a week later on Super Tuesday, Feb. 5, when voters in California, New York, New Jersey, Illinois and 16 other states voted in what was the equivalent of a national primary. Therefore, he looked to simply survive in the four early states and reserve enough money to do campaign advertising in the big states that voted later.

Ultimately the Giuliani strategy proved fatal when the other candidates built up momentum and gained media exposure that he lost by sitting in Florida waiting for them. In the Iowa primary, Mike Huckabee won 30% of the delegates, Mitt Romney 27% and McCain and Thompson both got 12%, although Thompson won more delegates. Giuliani finished sixth and last with 6%. In New Hampshire, both opportunity and fear led him to campaign more seriously. On the positive side, his strategists determined that Giuliani was not too far behind the other candidates to be competitive. But he also decided that ignoring the early states was too risky. Thus he waged an intensive radio campaign and sent at least 8 direct mail pieces to voters. In spite of the expenditure of considerable resources, Giuliani placed 4th in the state, which McCain won by 37% to 32% over Romney, with Huckabee in third place.

Florida came fully into play in the aftermath of the New Hampshire race, when Giuliani skipped the primaries in Michigan and South Carolina and the caucuses in Nevada in order to focus on the Sunshine State primary. His strategy was to use Florida as a "launch pad" for a strong showing in the March 2 Super Tuesday. In the meantime, the other candidates went to Michigan, where Romney, whose father was a former governor, won, keeping him in the race, and to South Carolina where McCain's victory over Huckabee solidified his role as the candidate to beat and gave him momentum going into Florida. With both Romney and Thompson gaining votes in South Carolina, McCain was able to narrowly defeat Huckabee and to demonstrate that he could unite the party.

Giuliani, reputedly banking on a July 2007 endorsement commitment from Governor Charlie Crist, (Chalian. 2010) had focused on Florida since the days immediately following the state's changing of its primary date and had staff in place there beginning in the early part of 2007. From December 24, 2007 until January 29th, Giuliani devoted substantial amounts of money and considerable time to Florida, campaigning with almost no on-the-ground opposition until after the South Carolina race on February 3. During this time, he spent money every week on television, totaling $2, 975,975 on 4, 246 spots. (TNSmedia intelligence/cmag) Florida was the first state in which only Republicans were voting in the closed primary, forcing all candidates to tailor their message to the fiscal and social conservatives who dominate the party in the State. To attract this constituency, Giuliani's primary message was tax reduction, claiming that on his first day in office as president, he would send Congress the largest tax cut in history, but he also trumpeted his actions as Mayor of New York after the 9/11 attacks as evidence that he could deal with terrorism. In the last week before election day, he spent $1.1 million on 1,445 television ads in Florida promoting these messages.

Mitt Romney's campaign in Florida had also begun early and was well organized and well financed, to a considerable extent with his own money. He had planned on competing in an October Republican straw poll ultimately canceled by the state's governor and for months had more than a dozen staff members based in Florida. Enough of these came from the staff of former governor Jeb Bush that it generated speculation that Bush was supporting him. These people included Sally Bradshaw, Bush chief of staff and campaign manager and Al Cardenas, RPOF Chair during Bush's first term. Romney's statewide steering committee was composed of other people close to Jeb Bush; well known former office holders and political activists such as the former Secretary of State and former Mayor of Orlando, Glenda Hood, the former Lt. Governor, Toni Jennings, former Speakers of the House Alan Bense and John Thrasher and U.S. Congressman Tom Feeney. In 2007, Romney spent $2.5 million in Florida and was spending $567,000 a week in the period December 24, 2007 through primary election day. Over the full course of his Florida campaign he spent close to $5.3 million on roughly 5,700 television ads and in the last week of the campaign he spent $1.9 million on television. (TNSmedia intelligence) He campaigned as an experienced business leader who could deal better with the economy than other candidates and as the "true conservative" in the state. This stance earned him the support of Rush Limbaugh, the self-proclaimed "moral and intellectual leader of the Republican Party" both in Florida and in the nation.

Throughout the campaign, public opinion polls routinely showed John McCain close to the lead in Florida. Nevertheless, his organization struggled constantly. Financially, he trailed both Romney and Giuliani and his expenditures for television were well below those for both men, putting out just $2 million, all in the time period January 21–29. His support for the War in Iraq and his role in crafting the Republican plan for immigration reform were cited as reasons for his relatively poor showing. Thus he focused heavily on areas in the state where his message of national security would play well, like Tampa and the Panhandle—home to thousands of military personnel and their families.

Despite his organizational troubles, the victories in New Hampshire and, particularly, in South Carolina, and the earned media he garnered in these two states kept McCain's campaign alive, and in the final week before the primary vote both the Republican U.S. Senator, Mel Martinez, and the state's popular governor Charlie Crist endorsed him, along with some influential newspapers. FOX News exit polls seemed to indicate that the endorsements helped as McCain led among those who said that Crist's endorsement mattered. This was particularly galling to Giuliani who had been promised the Crist endorsement earlier in the campaign. (Balz and Johnson. 2009. 291)

The other "serious" candidate in the Florida Republican primary was Mike Huckabee, former Governor of Arkansas. There was potential for Huckabee in the state where social and religious conservatives are important constituencies, and where the closed Republican primary helps conservative candidates.

Furthermore, he did get the endorsement of several important conservative officials, two former Speakers of the Florida House of Representatives, Marco Rubio and Daniel Webster and of another Hispanic legislator, David Rivera. However, he was never able to raise the money necessary to conduct a plausible campaign in a huge state that requires millions of dollars to pay for television advertisements and travel. In addition, his loss to McCain in South Carolina undermined his claim as "the" conservative candidate. In the weeks just prior to the primary he was forced to ask some senior staff to work without pay, cut others from the payroll and severely restrict his travel plans. He bought no television ads in the state and was forced to rely on "earned media." In the end, his staff was reduced to hoping that the departure of Fred Thompson from the race after his loss in South Carolina would rebound in his favor.

Opinion polls in Florida as early as May, 2006 had Rudy Giuliani ahead in Florida. (Quinnipiac Poll. 2/15–20/06) And he maintained this lead until January, 2008. As the other major candidates opened their campaigns in the state, their support waxed and waned, with first Huckabee and then Romney gaining strength early in January. After the South Carolina primary, the polls, shown in Figure 2.1, indicated that John McCain was gaining strength, running slightly ahead of Mitt Romney, with Giuliani falling into a distant third. In the end, that is the way the election turned out. McCain got 36% of the vote, Romney 31%, Giuliani 15% and Mike Huckabee finished with 14%.

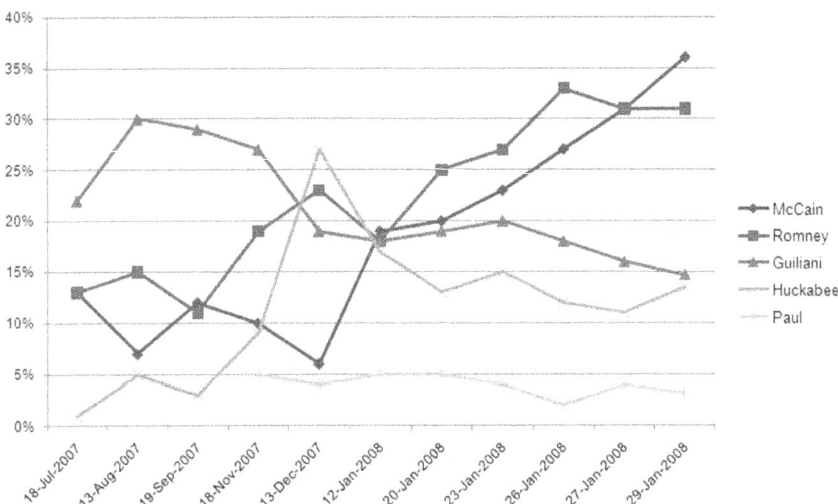

Figure 2.1. The Battle for the Republican Nomination in Florida: Rasmussen tracking pools leading up to the Republican primary in Florida.

Since the Republicans utilize a winner take all system for assignment of delegates, none of those who trailed McCain benefited in the delegate count.

McCain won 45 of the state's 67 counties, with 18 going to Romney and 4 to Huckabee. Despite his considerable effort in the Sunshine State, Giuliani won no counties. McCain won large margins in Miami-Dade, where Cuban Americans helped give him a 37,000 vote margin, overwhelming Romney by 48% to 14%. He was also helped by big margins in the Tampa Bay area where military and retired voters turned out in large numbers. Romney carried Orange County (Orlando) and northern portions of Florida (Duval) as well as wealthy counties such as Collier (Naples), but the margins were not large enough to offset the McCain vote in Miami-Dade. Huckabee wins came in the southern-accented counties in the "Old South" North Florida.

Exit polls showed that McCain's support came from Republican moderates, Hispanics and Florida's older Republicans. Hispanic voters were only 12% of the Republican electorate, but they voted 54% for McCain, with only 14% for Romney and 24% for Giuliani. More than half of McCain's 100,000 vote edge over Romney came in the Miami metropolitan area. Mitt Romney relied on solid support from conservatives and from those troubled by illegal immigration and abortion. He could not, however, convince people that he could get them out of the economic slump. Although he promoted his success as a business turnaround specialist, he fared badly among those Republicans who saw the US economy in crises. Exit polls showed this segment of the population voting for McCain, by 43 to 27 percent. Huckabee did no better than sharing the lead with Romney among white Christian evangelical and born-again voters, the group that had propelled him to victory in Iowa and which allegedly was his base.

The Florida primary proved pivotal in the 2008 Republican campaign and to some extent satisfied the interests of those who wanted to leverage Florida's importance in the presidential selection process. In the immediate aftermath of the primary, Giuliani dropped out of the race and endorsed McCain. Both Romney and Huckabee soldiered on. Romney capitulated after Super Tuesday on February 2, when McCain won twice as many delegates as his two rivals combined. But Huckabee ran until March 4, some said in order to win enough delegates to secure a prime speaking time at the Republican National Convention in order to boost his candidacy in 2012.

The Democrats

As the presidential campaign opened in 2007, Hillary Clinton was the leading Democratic candidate in the national polls. She led the race in virtually every poll taken until late in that year. In December, 2007, forty-two percent (42%) of likely voters supported her compared to 23% for Obama and 16% for Edwards. She also had a substantial lead in the superdelegate count.

As 2008 began, Clinton maintained what appeared to be a safe lead and Obama struggled to "build a campaign that was more than just an idea" while slogging through the debates with little success in breaking out from the pack. Then, on May 3, 2008, television personality Oprah Winfrey endorsed Mr. Obama on national television and went on a multi-state tour with him, including a December visit to Iowa. Social scientists claim that Winfrey's endorsement was responsible for approximately 1,000,000 additional votes for Obama, (Garthwaite and Moore. 2008) but Winfrey's endorsement may not have been the spur that energized the Obama campaign. Many political analysts and members of his own staff claim that Obama's outstanding performance in front of 10,000 people at the Iowa Democratic Party Jefferson-Jackson Day Dinner on November 10 was the tipping point for him. (Caeser, Busch and Pitney. 109) He began to gain ground thereafter and went on to win the Iowa caucus with 38% of the vote. Edwards finished second with 30% and Clinton came in third with 29%. Bill Richardson got 2% of the vote, Joe Biden won 1% and Chris Dodd got just under 1%. Biden and Dodd dropped out of the race and the others went on to New Hampshire where Clinton came back to claim a victory, followed by Obama and Edwards and forcing Richardson out. Clinton then won the popular vote in Nevada, but Obama won the caucuses in that state and the overall delegate count. Obama then had a huge victory in South Carolina where there was a large African-American population which turned out at a high level, forcing John Edwards to close his campaign, and Obama and Clinton headed toward what had originally been seen as definitive races in Florida and in the Super Tuesday contests. Yet the decision on the part of the DNC to discount the Florida outcome effectively took the state out of play at a critical point in the election and neither of the candidates actively campaigned there.

Despite the promises on the part of the candidates not to campaign in Florida, supporters of both Obama and Clinton did conduct unofficial campaigns and more than 350,000 individuals had cast early votes by the day before the primary. And not surprisingly, some of the usual kind of campaign conflict emerged. Two days before the election, Hillary Clinton visited Florida and held three fundraisers, which spurred complaints from Obama supporters. Then an Obama ad offended the Clinton team, simply because it was run. As an effort to influence voters in other states on Super Tuesday on February 5, the Obama campaign ran a nationwide television campaign that was shown in all states on CNN, including Florida. The Obama campaign asked that the ads not be run in Florida, but were told by the network that this was not possible and the ads ran.

In the absence of the candidates, the primary took place and a record number of Democrats voted. Nevertheless, there was lower voter turnout in that primary than in the Republican primary and much lower than in record-setting turnouts among Democrats in other states. Clinton won 49.7% of the delegates, Obama 32.9% and John Edwards won 14.3%. According to exit polls Clinton won virtually every demographic group with the exception of African-Americans; women, men, whites, Hispanics, and voters of all income and education levels. She then treated the outcome as if it had been a "real" contest by flying to Davie, Florida on election day to proclaim "a tremendous victory."

In the ensuing closely contested race various groups tried to negotiate a resolution to the standoff between the DNC and the Florida Democratic Party. Initially, the Clinton campaign called for the results to stand as counted. It subsequently asked for a new round of voting to take place. Her supporters argued that had her victory in Florida "counted," her subsequent wins in New York and California on Super Tuesday would have given her the momentum needed to win the necessary delegates to be the party's candidate in November. The Obama campaign refuted this, pointing out that the two campaigns basically split the Super Tuesday vote, with Obama winning more states and more delegates.

Democrats throughout the nation worried that failure to resolve the problem would lead to trouble at the National Convention that could have repercussions in the general election. The decision went to the DNC and on May 31, it voted to seat all of Florida's delegates according to the primary results, but to give them half votes. Later, when Obama became the presumptive nominee and determined that he could win the nomination with the votes as cast in Florida and in Michigan, he asked that all delegates be given full privileges. The DNC acceded to this request, the delegates were seated with full voting rights and a majority voted for Obama.

Nevertheless, Obama's campaign manager David Plouffe told a group at Harvard University after the campaign "if that Florida primary, coming three days after South Carolina, happened, it might have mitigated all the momentum we got from South Carolina. In fact, we might not be the nominee." (Balz and Johnson. 2008. 219)

SUMMARY

The Florida primaries proved pivotal for both political parties. It affected momentum for both candidates and it demonstrated to future candidates the implications of a calendar change and of a closed primary. McCain's win in the Republican race propelled him on to success on Super Tuesday and combined with his wins in these states proved decisive for him. It signified that Republicans throughout the nation were behind his candidacy.

By many accounts, the absence of a recognized Democratic primary in Florida also proved decisive for Barack Obama. Had the results produced in the unofficial primary been counted at the time as if they were official results, it is at least possible that Hillary Clinton would have been the Democratic nominee.

Chapter Three

The General Election in Florida

THE STRATEGIC CONTEXT

While Florida is the nation's fourth largest state and casts 27 electoral votes and is therefore always an important battleground, in 2008 it was more critical to the Republicans than to the Democrats. Given the national distribution of the two party vote, there were a number of scenarios in which the Democrats could have won the Presidency without winning Florida, but there were no such scenario for the Republicans; if they lost Florida they lost the election. Thus, there was a different imperative for the two parties in the presidential election.

On the ground, political conditions favored the Republicans. Florida is nominally a Democratic state, with both higher voter registration numbers and higher partisan identification figures for that Party, and in the previous two presidential cycles the Democratic presidential candidate had been highly competitive there. Nevertheless, the state's electorate is predominantly conservative, and Republicans held four of the six statewide elective positions and sixty-four percent (64%) of both the Congressional and the state legislative seats. In addition, the Democrats had last won a presidential election in Florida in 1996, and the Republicans had won eight of the previous ten presidential elections. Thus, the conventional wisdom was that Florida was a tough state for Democrats to win, so difficult that some critics of the McCain campaign said later that Republicans bought into this belief and took the state for granted until late in the campaign.

POSITIONING, TARGETING AND MESSAGE

The presidential candidates in 2008 focused their campaigns on geographic areas of the state that had been favorable to their respective parties in previous elections and on specific groups that had been their supporters. For the Republicans these areas were West Florida (Pensacola to Fort Walton Beach), Southwest Florida (Naples, Fort Myers and the Western Everglades) and Northeast Florida and Jacksonville. Their "base" constituencies were hard-core conservatives, Hispanics in Miami, wealthy retirees and the military. Democratic strongholds are in South Florida (Miami-Dade, Broward and Palm Beach counties), and in North Central Florida, particularly in Leon County, the state capital, and in the small rural counties that surround it, and in Alachua County, home of the University of Florida. The Democratic constituencies are urbanites in Miami and Palm Beach, African Americans, young people and, increasingly, Puerto Ricans and other non-Cuban Hispanics. The "battleground" of the state lies in the area along the I-4 corridor which runs from Daytona Beach to the Tampa area. The 10-county Tampa Bay media market, the state's largest, holds the highest share of the state's independent voters.

To appeal to these Florida voters, both John McCain and Barack Obama articulated the messages used in their national campaigns, with minor adjustments for local circumstances. Obama organized the state into five regions in order to center attention on regional issues sometimes lost in state-wide campaigns. In Miami, he campaigned on "health care and Cuba. On the Space Coast it was Obama's plan for protecting NASA from budget cuts and in the Panhandle, the campaign pitched a proposal to end water wars with Georgia that were crippling the seafood industry." (Klas. 2008. Nov. 8)

McCain began by trying to capitalize on his long record of military service and his support of strong measures to protect the nation against terrorism. He assumed that this record would have particularly strong appeal in a state like Florida which has a large number of both social conservatives and active and retired military personnel. He also sought to portray Obama as too inexperienced to assume the job of being president and of being a liberal elitist who was out of touch with average, working Americans. Promoting a simpler message, Barack Obama made "change" the central theme of his campaign, focused attention on economic matters and tried to tie John McCain to George Bush.

Over the course of the campaign Barack Obama remained consistent in the way in which he positioned himself and in articulating his message. Once he chose change as his organizing theme, he stuck with it. When his opponent attacked him on his lack of experience, his associations with controversial figures and his political philosophy, he stayed on message. The message was that "the Bush policies had failed, that McCain was essentially carrying the tattered banner of a failed administration and that we represented a change from that." (Lizza. 2008) In addition, Obama worked to build his support among non-Cuban Hispanics, to ensure that the Republicans did not cut the Jewish vote out from under him and to demonstrate to the people living in rural Central Florida and the Panhandle that his comments about "bitter" voters "clinging to guns and religion" were not meant to disparage them.

John McCain faced a different, and arguably more difficult, challenge when positioning himself. He needed the Republican base of social conservatives and evangelicals and could not break completely from President Bush without antagonizing these groups. However, because the President was unpopular with other segments of the electorate he needed some way to distance himself from him. Thus, he projected a somewhat muddled message that sometimes emphasized his "maverick" credentials, sometimes his experience and sometimes his conservatism. Even his allies complained that the campaign "has offered myriad confusing themes that lurch between pitching McCain as a committed conservative one day and an independent-minded reformer the next, while displaying little of the focus that characterized President Bush's successful campaigns." (Stone. 2008. June 25) Furthermore, Obama's relentless focus on change distracted McCain from talking about his own strengths; his track record, his experience and his relationships with world leaders.

HOW THE DEMOCRATS CAMPAIGNED: THE GROUND GAME

Steve Schale, a long time political operative for the Florida Democratic Party who became the State Director for the Obama Campaign, interviewed for his job on June 3, 2008. In that meeting he was forced to spend some time arguing that Florida was winnable and refuting the thinking by some national Democratic strategists that the state be "downgraded" to secondary status in order to concentrate resources in other areas. At the time, both Pennsylvania and Michigan were thought to be in play and neither could be lost if the Democrats were to win. Ultimately, Schale's argument was successful; he was hired on June 16 and set off to put together the Florida component of Obama for America.

The ban on campaigning in Florida during the Democratic primary carried some negative consequences for that Party but one positive effect for Obama was the creation of strong grassroots organizations in the state. Without any help, or interference, from the national campaign, volunteers took on full responsibility for getting a campaign up and running and by the time the national campaign got involved there was already in existence a large, enthusiastic organic campaign on behalf of Barack Obama. Terry Watson had created the Tampa Bay O-Train in Hillsborough County and had organized between 5 and 6 thousand volunteers, sending over 100 volunteers to states other than Florida in the primaries, and similar organizations, such as Orlando4Obama, Tallahassee for Obama, and Miami4Obama had sprung up around the state. Florida's Obama team, Obama for America, took advantage of these existing organization, brought them into their own orbit and supported their activities. Obama for America paid the salaries of the State Director and the Field Director. Obama's chief national strategist David Axelrod recognized the value of these organizations and said they "gave us an enormous head start." (Kennedy School of Government. 2009. 98)

In addition to these two organizations, the state Democratic Party had been pointing toward the '08 election since 2004 and many county parties, such as those in Jefferson, Duval, Palm Beach and others, had already begun voter identification activities. In 2008, the Democrats changed the names of its traditional state legislative campaign organizations—House and Senate Victory—and consolidated them into the Florida Campaign for Change—a grassroots, voter contact organization paid for by the Democratic National Committee. Thus, multiple campaign activities were in place and multiple offices opened in some areas such as Tampa Bay. The Democrats claimed that the three organizations were controlled centrally and that they constituted the "largest and most aggressive voter outreach program in the history of our state." (Levitt. 2008)

The campaign took some criticism for its decision to use on-going organizations initiated by individuals who had not been screened by campaign officials or who were not directly connected to Obama for America, fearing they might be hard to manage and control. However, the Obama team had watched John Kerry's 2004 campaign use huge amounts of time vetting staff and fall behind in putting people in place throughout the state. Thus they were determined to have staff on the ground even if it meant that they were more loosely screened than deemed ideal.

This decision produced a variety of organizational problems and conflict between the grassroots organizations and the paid CFC staff was, initially at least, fairly widespread. Financial management proved particularly vexing. The Florida Democratic Party and the Campaign for Change relied on each other for financial information, but most of those hired by CFC were selected for their expertise as field organizers and were provided little or no training in the intricacies of preparing payroll reports or in reporting campaign contributions and expenditures. Furthermore, the CFC headquarters were located in Tampa, but all financial transactions and staffing paperwork was channeled through the FDP in Tallahassee. While no major problems emerged, one staff "insider" said that the campaign and the Florida Democratic Party sustained thousands of dollars in fines for late submission of financial reports.

Utilizing the three organizations and spurred by great personal enthusiasm for the candidate, Obama for America opened between 40 and 50 offices throughout the state in the six weeks after June 16. In August of 2008, nearly 200 paid staffers were on board and by the end of the campaign, the Democrats had approximately 250,000 volunteers, 350 paid staff and employees working out of about 100 offices located throughout the state, using an active e-mail list of 650,000 names. (Stratton. 2008; *Newsweek*. 2008.)

In addition to these campaign-related organizations, specialized groups were created to reach out to particular segments of the state's electorate. Two examples were the Florida Women for Obama and the Jewish Community Leadership Committees. Florida Women for Obama included 39,000 members who hosted over 4,000 events for the campaign and raised about $350,000. (Harfoush. 2009. 82) And six Jewish Community Leadership Committees (JCLCs) were established, comprising nearly 1000 Jewish leaders across the state in Miami, Broward County, Palm Beach County, Tampa Bay, Orlando and Sarasota. The committees were to concentrate on reaching Jewish voters in synagogues and Jewish organizations. They were created out of concern that Jewish voters would be wary of voting for a black candidate and to counter the fearmongering from conservatives about how Obama was a Muslim and supposedly anti-Israel.

The campaign for Jewish votes was augmented by an independent effort initiated by Ari Wallach, co-executive director of Jews Vote, a Jewish advocacy group. Calling on comedian Sarah Silverman, the group made a case for Obama in a web video that was marketed as the "Great Schlep." The video ended with Silverman urging Obama supporters to tell their grandparents in Florida that a failure to vote for Obama would result in no visits from their grandchildren. This video became a web sensation, producing about 2 million hits in the first two weeks after its posting. Thousands of people said they would call their grandparents and over 100 volunteered to pay their own way to Florida to campaign for Obama among Jewish voters. (Opperman. 2008)

In pursuing its mobilization goals, the Obama campaign is credited with creating a new form of political organization, allocated throughout five regions, or "pods," each with its own field staff and message geared to regional concerns. As described by the Director of the Media Lab of the ad holding company Havas, Obama's organization was neither tall nor flat, the two traditional structures, but "spherical—a tightly controlled core, surrounded by self-organizing cells of volunteers, donors, contributors and other participants at the fuzzy edges." (Haque. 2008)

Drawing on Obama's experience as a community organizer, the campaign spurned the traditional precinct captain model and focused instead on building volunteer teams of five or six members under the direction of a "neighborhood team leader." These volunteers assumed specific, clearly defined roles, including data coordinator, volunteer recruitment, phone-bank management and canvassing. They reported to a paid field director, were given quantifiable goals and were assigned to a specific "turf" within their "pod." Harnessing social networking on the Internet and cell phones, these teams were encouraged to recruit new coordinators and to build new teams, thus expanding their reach. Team members were provided training in the nuts and bolts of modern targeted campaigning and were given access to the high-tech information management tools that are now indispensable to voter contact operations. Perhaps the most important of these was VoteBuilder, the State Democratic Party's voter database. Access to this database was provided to Obama's neighborhood teams, along with permission to update it to reflect the ongoing contact activities. They also utilized a web site, voteforchange.com to walk potential voters through registration, polling locations and early voting instructions.

As one Obama staffer explained it, the neighborhood teams were self-reliant, self-sufficient and required very little in the way of staff support. (Sizemore. 2008) Their creation permitted many of the time consuming "clerical" aspects of campaigning such as cutting up target areas, pulling lists of voters, putting canvass packets together, and calling voters, to be done in a more manageable fashion and in a more convenient place for volunteers to get to. The organization also gave ownership in the campaign to more volunteers and contributed to volunteer enthusiasm. One thousand four hundred and fourteen (1,414) of these teams were created, and a total of 22,000 volunteers were formally involved. (Klas. 2008)

The primary tasks for the organization were to identify Democratic voters, get them registered and encourage them to vote early or by absentee ballot. This effort was broad based, but it paid particular attention to areas where Democrats had been less successful in previous presidential campaigns. The state campaign reasoned that Obama would maximize the existing vote in heavily Democratic counties such as Miami-Dade and Broward and that it would be able to add to the 2004 vote total in those counties. They were afraid, however, that this would not be enough to offset what was expected to be a strong push by Republicans, who had a history of getting their voters to the polls. Thus they sought to build support in less Democratic counties, even if they might lose them, and in particular in the counties where there had been some population change since 2004. And the campaign had the volunteers to do this. Therefore, the campaign worked hard in places like Duval, Hillsborough and Pinellas counties where Kerry had lost in 2004. Many of the appearances of campaign principals, Obama, his wife Michele and vice presidential candidate Joe Biden took place in these areas; so many that some Democrats complained that they were ignoring "base" counties.

The Obama ground game achieved great success; it registered more new voters than did McCain and was more successful in reaching early and absentee voters. In the four months preceding the November election, the campaign registered 200,000 new voters in Florida, recruited 600,000 volunteers and allocated about $40 million to support its candidate. (Klas. 2008) By the end of the campaign someone from the Obama organization had either called or talked to in person more than 15% of those who voted in the 2008 election in Florida, over twice the number contacted by the Republicans. (MSMBC. 2008)

HOW THE DEMOCRATS CAMPAIGNED: THE AIR WARS

Obama's ground game was supported by "the greatest torrent of advertising Florida has ever seen." (Deslatte and Stratton. 2008) He saturated radio and TV, buying ads throughout the full campaign period. According to TNS Media Intelligence which monitors political advertising on television, Obama spent $36 million in Florida on television alone. He purchased 32,562 gross rating points between June 11 and November 4, 2008. (Huang and Shaw, 2009)

Ad "story boards" obtained from TNS Media Intelligence showed that the Obama television campaign employed a fairly conventional "dual track" strategy, combining both positive and negative ads. "Negative" ads are those that attack an opponent's policies or personal characteristics. "Positive" ads extol the virtues of a candidate's own policies or characteristics without demeaning the opposition and "comparative" ads provide straightforward descriptions of the differences between the positions of the candidates on various issues. (Mark. 2009)

Between September and November 4, the Obama dual track strategy led the campaign to spend almost equally on positive and negative ads, with slightly more money on the negative spots. The totals were $9.6 million negative to $9.5 million positive. Over $2.5 million ($2,673,035) was devoted to "comparative" ads that contrasted Obama's medical plan with that of McCain and that compared the candidates' competing tax proposals.

The "negative" ads utilized by the Obama campaign were of two kinds; attempts to tie McCain to President George Bush and direct attacks on positions Senator McCain had taken over the years or had proposed during the 2008 campaign. None of the ads were direct personal attacks on the Senator's character or morals.

In a commercial entitled "Look Behind," Obama claimed that John McCain "wants to continue George Bush's economic policies." In "No Third Term," he asked "do we want another eight years of what we just went through? If you want another eight years, just stay at home." And in another ad called "Same," he depicted President Bush and Senator McCain in an embrace with the caption "they share the same out-of-touch attitude; the same failure to understand the economy; the same tax cuts for huge corporations and the wealthiest one percent." It ended with McCain shown saying "I voted with the president over 90 percent of the time. Higher than, uh, a lot of my, uh, even Republican colleagues," and the announcer saying "we just can't afford more of the same."

The more direct negative attacks focused on McCain policy proposals and campaign tactics. In a commercial with the title "Audio Tapes", Obama said that while the nation was in an economic meltdown, John McCain was "playing with audio tapes," referring to a McCain ad that had quoted Joe Biden saying that "the next president will be tested," but leaving out the remainder of the statement, which was "they're gonna find out this guy's got steel in his spine." In more direct attacks, as in "Floridians Hurting," Obama criticized McCain's statement that "the fundamentals of our economy are strong," and in "Golden Years" raised the question "how would your golden years turn out under John McCain?" suggesting that Medicare would be cut by 22%, that there would more expensive prescription drugs under a McCain presidency and that "after a lifetime of work, seniors' health care shouldn't be a gamble." Finally, in "Need Education" and "Looking Out For," Obama ads appealed to women by pointing out that McCain had come out against "equal pay for equal work," and for opposing "our right to choose."

In Obama's positive ads, the candidate reminisced about his mother and her father and how they had instilled in him the values of "hard work, honesty...kindness, faith." In "Defining Moment," he asked for the vote of the American people and said that "if we stand together, we can meet our challenges and ensure that there are better days ahead," and in "Florida is Rich," he extolled the virtue of Florida's diverse culture, said he understood this culture and the aspirations of the people and said "together we can realize the promise of our country."

Overall, the Obama campaign organization performed at a superior level, both on the ground and in the air and at the end of the campaign, even the

Republicans complemented them. Sally Bradshaw, campaign manager for former Governor Jeb Bush said "They've done everything right ... They've broken the code." (Klas. 2008) And former state Republican chairman, Tom Slade, said "Bar none. He has the best political organization for a presidential campaign I have ever seen here." (Lizza. 2008)

HOW THE REPUBLICANS CAMPAIGNED: THE GROUND GAME

When John McCain won the Super Tuesday primaries and wrapped up the Republican nomination, he was in a strong position to enhance his national organization and to raise the money he needed to compete in Florida against Barack Obama who was still engaged in a grueling primary contest with Clinton that would continue into late May. However, when the RPOF and the McCain organization held their first meeting after Super Tuesday, one participant reported that the presidential campaign had classified Florida as a "safe" state that would require only minimal attention. An effort was made to dissuade the McCain organization of this notion by drawing a comparison between the Bush Victory effort in 2000, when Florida was initially characterized as a "safe" state only to end up with alarm bells in October and a protracted voter recount, to that in 2004 when the Party competed all out from the outset of the campaign. But the McCain organization, constrained by a difficult national electoral map and campaign budget, postponed a decision until it was too late and did not take appropriate advantage of this time period.

To compete in the general election, John McCain had to overcome a serious problem that plagued him throughout the campaign and that surfaced during the primaries, weak on-the-ground organization. This weakness was glaringly displayed in Florida. Despite his victory in the Sunshine State primary, the McCain campaign never had a strong ground operation in Florida. To some extent, a "loosely organized and sometime ad hoc approach to campaigning has been part of Sen. McCain's persona." (Holmes and Williamson. 2008) But more importantly, the Senator simply could not raise the money necessary to compete throughout the nation. As early as July of 2007, the national campaign suffered such poor fundraising totals that it was forced to lay off dozens of staffers and aides, including those specifically assigned to Florida. In that same month a co-chairman of the Florida campaign was arrested on charges of soliciting a sex act from an undercover law enforcement officer. Thus, to the extent to which he had a ground campaign in Florida during the primary it was managed by volunteers. (Sharockman. 2007) And it "lagged far behind what both Romney and Giuliani had in Florida," both of whom had paid staff in place for months and were supplemented with staff from other states. (Martin. 2008)

In the immediate aftermath of the Florida primary, the small McCain organization left the state in order to continue efforts in the Super Tuesday primaries and in other races and it was not until the end of April that it returned. In early May, there was still only one full-time staff member working the whole state and one consultant in place in South Florida and the first McCain field offices were not opened until June. By contrast, in March, 2004, the Bush campaign had opened field offices statewide and begun test driving their ground operation. Thus, the McCain campaign was unable to implement the proven Republican game plan and it was not until July that the organization was fully staffed. It was not until the end of August that the Republican state party organization, GOP Victory, was also fully operational, and the two organizations shared office space at the Tallahassee headquarters of the Republican Party of Florida (RFOP).

Despite their physical proximity, the McCain organization and that of the Republican Party of Florida endured a somewhat shaky relationship. The McCain campaign believed that popular Governor Charlie Crist would be able to deliver the state without significant national resources. The political people at the state party believed the McCain effort was a ghost from campaigns past and dubbed it Dole, part II.

The Republican Party in Florida has always had a strong "ground game" and has been credited with writing the voter mobilization playbook that helped turn Karl Rove into a political superstar. (Smith. 2008*)* The GOP has been particularly effective in getting Republicans who are registered to vote actually to go to the polls. However, in Florida in 2008, McCain was criticized for underutilizing this machine, and critics said that his "national campaign staff did a dismal job of coordinating" with it. (Padgett. 2008) The GOP chair in Pasco County, said "Pasco is hitting on all cylinders," but added "I don't want to step on anybody's toes, but the Bush campaign was probably better organized." (Stratton. 2008) To some extent this type of friction is endemic to political campaigns, particularly when a candidate is struggling, but the rumblings were widespread enough to prompt an October meeting in Tallahassee where Republican Party officials aired their grievances and a former Republican state chair said "I get the sense that on a statewide basis, the grass roots Republicans don't quite feel like they have a natural fit with the McCain organization." (*The Reid Report.* 2008)

Despite their disagreements, toward the final weeks of the campaign the Republicans mounted their usual high level ground campaign. The RPOF claimed to have led the nation in the number of volunteer contacts in six of the final seven weeks of the 2008 election cycle. The Party installed upgraded phone systems with advanced data capture methods to better target voters and launched a text message program to contact volunteers and voters. In addition, Florida Republicans created a new Absentee Ballot Request Walk Program and implemented absentee chase efforts that were adopted by the national party. "Through extensive volunteer efforts, the RPOF contacted more than four million voters in 2008, more than ever before. During the 2008 GOTV Program, volunteers made over one million phone calls and knocked on more than 100,000 doors." (Republican Party of Florida. 2009)

MSMBC exit polls suggested that through their efforts the Republicans contacted about 7.2% of those who voted in the 2008 election or over 800,000 individuals. This was a substantial number, but it was less than half the number that MSMBC said had been contacted by the Democrats. (MSMBC. 2008)

HOW THE REPUBLICANS CAMPAIGNED: THE AIR WARS

Constrained as it was by a relative shortage of money and a strategic decision to accept federal matching funds, McCain's television campaign in Florida paled in comparison to that of Obama. During the time period when Obama was spending over $36 million in the state, McCain and allies of the candidate, the RNC, the National Republican Trust PAC and the Republican Jewish Coalition purchased 15,082 gross rating points at a cost of $17, 133,501. (TMSMediaIntelligence) The McCain media effort was dwarfed by the size and scope of the Obama campaign.

Despite pressure from the state party to air positive ads featuring popular incumbent Governor Charlie Crist, perhaps sensing that Obama was gaining momentum around the nation and concerned about protecting a must-win state from the Democrats, McCain adopted a "single track" strategy, and utilized his television campaign in Florida exclusively to attack Barack Obama. The ad story boards provided by TNS Media Intelligence showed that not one spot run between September and November 4 identified a proposal to resolve a policy problem facing the nation or gave voters a reason for supporting McCain, aside from pointing out the limitations of his opponent. During the first three weeks of the general election in Florida, McCain spent $3,227,260 on 3,784 spots, all of them negative attack ads. One ad called "Dome" attacked Obama and liberal allies for favoring "massive government," "wasteful pork," and "painful income taxes, sky-rocketing taxes on life savings." Another, entitled "Ambition," claimed that Obama was "blinded by ambition" and "when convenient he worked with terrorist Bill Ayers. When discovered he lied." And a third, entitled "Unethical," said "Obama rewards his friends with your tax dollars. That's unethical."

In the final three weeks of the campaign, McCain's efforts to raise questions about Obama's character, his experience and his policies continued and he spent another $2,047,340 on 3,678 negative attack ads. In this period he brought in former governor Jeb Bush to ask "do we elect a President who will raise your taxes?' "Spread your income?" "Spend us deeper into debt?" He ran Spanish language ads claiming that "Obama and his Congressional allies support abortions for underage girls without the permission of their parents and oppose mandatory sentences for sexual predators, drug dealers and rapists." And he made extensive use of the "Joe the Plumber," character who had wandered into the McCain campaign and become a spokesman for the candidate. In these ads different people say things like "Obama wants my sweat to pay for his trillion dollars in new spending," and "Spread the wealth?: I'm supposed to work harder just to pay more taxes?" ending these statements with "I'm Joe the Plumber."

As the campaign came to a close, the McCain television effort was augmented by support from the Republican National Committee, the National Republican Trust PAC and the Republican Jewish Coalition. These organizations also adopted the single track negative strategy employed by the McCain campaign and spent $5,569,365 on 7,718 ads. The RNC ads all criticized Obama's lack of experience, the Republican Jewish Coalition ran excerpts from the Democratic primary debates in which Hillary Clinton called Obama's willingness to meet separately with leaders of Iran, Syria and other countries "irresponsible," and the Republican Trust PAC ran an ad called "Preacher of Hate," which featured the well publicized comments of Obama's longtime minister Jeremiah Wright saying "not God bless America. God damn America." This ad was run 236 times between October 27 and election day on November 4.

In the end, John McCain, a man who had once said that candidates who ran negative ads were candidates who had no ideas of their own, became one of those candidates in Florida. Later in the book, we examine the proposition that this strategy may have alienated one segment of the electorate.

Chapter Four

The Election Results

As the presidential primaries came to a close, Barack Obama and John McCain were virtually tied in national presidential preference polls. Between the time of the Democratic convention on August 25–28 and the Republican Convention on September 1–4, Obama gained an advantage that was briefly lost in the aftermath of the Republican Convention, and on September 7 fell behind John McCain by 5 points in the Gallup Daily tracking poll. This was the last time that McCain held a lead in the race. While his margin was never very large, Obama regained the lead a week later and was consistently ahead in the race thereafter. In the week before the election, the Gallup Poll expanded election model gave him a lead of 51% to 44%.

In Florida, the circumstances were almost reversed. In 26 polls conducted from late 2007 until August, 2008, McCain led in all but 5. Beginning on September 13, 2008 Obama gained ground and in the 27 polls conducted from that point until November 2, traded the lead with McCain. The margins between the two candidates decreased as the election neared and on November 2, the day before the election, the Rasmussen Poll shown in Figure 4.1 put McCain ahead.

It was against this backdrop that Floridians tuned into election night television coverage of the campaign with fear and trepidation. And it was not until relatively late in the evening that the anxiety was resolved. At 11:13 pm the Associated Press projected the Florida election as a victory for Senator Obama, solidifying an earlier pronouncement by the networks that he would win the national election. Both Floridians and the nation at large took a breath, the Democrats celebrated and the Republicans lamented their fate.

In the final Florida tally, Obama amassed 4,282,074 votes to 4,045,624 for McCain, a victory of 51.4% of the vote to 48.6%. This election broke a string of Republican presidential victories in Florida that stretched back to Bill

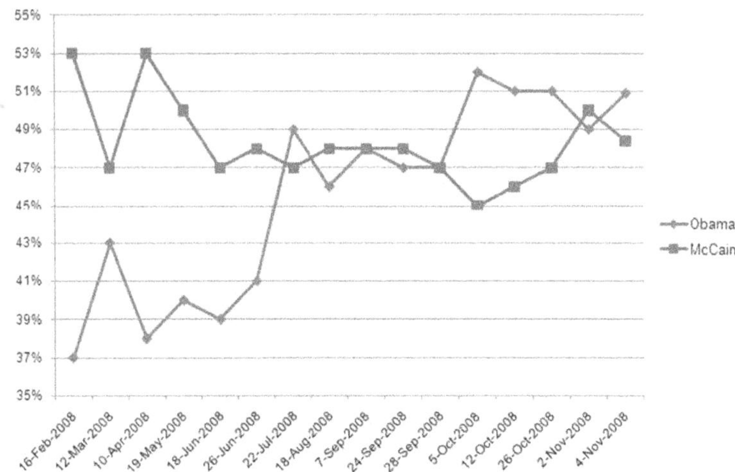

Figure 4.1. The Battle for Florida: Rasmussen tracking polls leading up to the presidential election in Florida.

Clinton's second term and it was only the third time that the Democrats had won the presidential election in the state since Lyndon Johnson won in 1964.

The margin of victory in Florida (2.8%) was well below the 7.2% margin Obama achieved at the national level and was the third smallest in all the presidential elections in Florida since 1980. Only the tie between Bush/Chaney and Gore/Lieberman in 2000 and the 1.9% loss of Clinton/Gore to Bush/Quayle in 1992 had smaller margins. Obama won only 15 of the state's 67 counties.

One of the striking features of the 2008 election was the similarity of the physical location of the vote with that in 2004. Although the overall outcome was different, only 4 counties voted differently in 2008 than they had in 2004. Nevertheless, these four were important and Obama picked up over half of his victory total (132, 701 votes) in these four turnarounds. They were Osceola, Hillsborough, Pinellas and Flagler. All had voted for Bush/Chaney in 2004, but went for Obama/Biden in 2008. His other gains over Kerry and Liberman came through increased Democratic turnout in the other counties, even those he lost.

EARLY AND ABSENTEE VOTING

In 2008, Florida was one of 36 states in the nation that allowed early voting, which increases convenience for voters and reduces election day stress for electoral officials. It was initiated in response to the chaos surrounding the highly contentious fight over the tightly contested 2000 presidential election and was designed to remedy some of the problems that emerged in that election. The thinking was that early voting would make lines shorter and make it easier to provide individual assistance to voters who required it. Further, it would reduce the number of disputes and permit resolution of ambiguity with ballots in a less stressful environment. Early voting in Florida includes in person voting where voters cast ballots at designated places well before election day and "no-excuse" absentee voting.

Beginning in 2002, county elections supervisors were allowed to offer early voting, but it was not required until 2004, when the legislature established a standard set of rules for early in-person voting. Walk in voting begins 15 days before the election and ends on the second day before the election. Initially the polling places were open eight hours each week day and eight additional hours over each weekend. During approximately the same time period, absentee ballots are mailed out and returned. In the first election in which these procedures were allowed in Florida, more than four million voters took advantage of them.

In the 2004 presidential election in Florida about one third of the votes cast in the election were cast early or by mail. According to an Associated Press analysis of these votes, the two candidates did about as well in this stage of the election as they did in the voting on election day. George Bush carried Florida by about 381,000 votes and beat John Kerry both in early voting and on Election Day. The differences were 4% in early voting and 5% on Election Day.

As the 2008 election season opened, it became apparent that the 2004 early voting numbers would be eclipsed. The turnout for early voting in 2008 was massive, approaching 50% of the registered vote in the state. Long waits in line were common and pressure developed to expand the time for citizens to cast early votes. In response, Republican Governor Charlie Crist, at some criticism from some in his Party who saw early voting as advantageous to Democrats, increased the time for early voting on weekdays by four hours and left up to county election officials decisions about longer hours on weekends.

The first required appearance of early voting in the 2004 general election drew in 1,428,362 votes cast at early voting sites across the state. Four years later during the 2008 election, the number of early votes in the state jumped to 2,661,672. Correctly anticipating the increased popularity in early voting, the Obama campaign devoted much time and money to galvanize the early vote among its supporters in Florida for the 2008 election. This vast ground operation seems to have helped Obama's early voting numbers in Florida: as shown in Table 4.1, Democrats cast a total of 1,534,087 early votes compared to Republicans' 917,378.

Table 4.1. Distribution of Early, Absentee, and Election Day Voting

	Election Day		Absentee		Early Voting	
	DEM	REP	DEM	REP	DEM	REP
Alachua	26,227	19,514	13,160	9,742	37,113	13,244
Baker	2,797	1,673	1,011	806	3,301	2,431
Bay	13,038	17,883	6,470	11,807	13,079	15,180
Bradford	3,444	2,368	1,069	888	2,888	1,851
Brevard	63,640	82,998	24,146	38,489	29,383	19,355
Broward	185,564	110,627	70,963	50,854	187,551	45,567
Calhoun	3,007	594	564	230	1,961	420
Charlotte	7,994	12,654	9,543	16,004	14,141	15,403
Citrus	11,937	14,606	6,639	10,408	12,274	12,329
Clay	10,807	27,035	3,705	11,063	13,932	23,741
Collier	13,895	31,684	8,314	24,799	18,141	27,382
Columbia	5,784	4,212	2,910	2,553	7,835	5,147
Desoto	2,828	1,475	1,126	850	2,675	1,104
Dixie	3,254	922	1,117	452	1,407	449
Duval	66,800	72,658	33,221	42,026	108,353	64,190
Escambia	27,304	34,017	14,098	22,852	26,668	20,281
Flagler	7,089	8,615	2,851	4,474	11,151	8,099
Franklin	2,255	558	1,098	455	1,630	459
Gadsden	7,812	1,546	2,628	747	9,613	1,199
Gilchrist	2,498	1,890	805	689	1,387	990
Glades	2,681	1,312	63	51	160	74
Gulf	1,856	1,000	848	575	2,372	1,178
Hamilton	2,366	547	913	312	1,271	353
Hardee	2,115	1,236	556	501	2,209	1,149
Hendry	2,800	1,813	950	836	3,248	1,830
Hernando	17,812	22,256	8,246	10,542	12,502	8,784
Highlands	6,468	8,867	2,722	5,291	10,224	9,231
Hillsborough	106,890	104,935	51,182	56,782	89,728	44,509
Holmes	3,270	1,330	1,201	687	1,933	865
Indian River	8,036	14,880	4,908	10,541	11,046	13,912
Jackson	8,400	3,149	2,320	1,390	5,413	1,982
Jefferson	3,023	968	869	453	2,459	751
Lafayette	1,494	418	442	151	861	252
Lake	21,164	32,736	10,066	18,365	25,898	25,833
Lee	39,433	65,866	23,887	47,960	29,664	28,177
Leon	47,393	26,510	17,241	11,655	34,526	9,935
Levy	6,266	3,684	2,427	2,010	3,075	1,400
Liberty	1,802	196	422	71	982	156
Madison	3,213	857	1,203	341	2,940	685
Manatee	33,894	48,307	12,013	21,104	12,165	7,570

While the GOP lagged behind in early voter turnout in 2008, it kept its footing in election day votes and absentee ballots. Republicans turned out to vote on election day slightly more than their Democrat counterparts, resulting in a total of 1,694,838 Republican votes on election day compared to 1,663,493 Democratic votes. In absentee voting, Republicans outvoted Democrats in 35 out of 67 counties in the absentee ballot category and returned a total of 12.8% more absentee ballots than Democratic voters.

Table 4.1. *(Continued)*

Marion	31,846	40,709	12,596	19,542	25,818	18,516
Martin	7,717	15,086	7,120	16,363	10,955	14,422
Miami-Dade	168,456	135,219	63,272	91,577	196,253	90,841
Monroe	5,717	6,883	5,156	6,665	6,864	5,358
Nassau	3,667	6,891	2,830	5,408	7,337	10,869
Okaloosa	10,714	27,409	4,382	15,579	10,593	21,238
Okeechobee	3,392	2,070	1,371	1,237	3,086	1,697
Orange	88,970	85,268	53,008	55,803	94,547	40,479
Osceola	21,496	17,710	6,429	7,791	25,476	12,589
Palm Beach	148,410	116,331	56,661	49,077	97,693	32,508
Pasco	42,610	52,346	14,088	21,620	33,448	26,924
Pinellas	97,604	103,805	73,731	83,492	31,081	14,554
Polk	55,773	59,726	21,850	29,114	36,520	19,330
Putnam	10,973	6,365	2,969	2,806	7,328	3,076
Santa Rosa	9,893	23,132	3,468	11,836	9,033	16,054
Sarasota	25,746	46,606	19,845	28,952	30,185	30,932
Seminole	30,502	44,822	13,510	26,827	38,939	31,371
St. Johns	10,575	23,240	5,615	14,272	17,423	28,856
St. Lucie	20,404	20,085	13,314	13,937	26,556	12,984
Sumter	4,950	5,970	2,779	5,610	11,087	14,479
Suwannee	5,854	3,150	2,055	1,547	3,690	1,778
Taylor	3,563	1,206	1,502	636	2,189	811
Union	1,924	860	1,006	372	1,041	510
Volusia	52,161	49,847	19,472	26,758	39,577	20,917
Wakulla	3,798	1,841	1,614	1,008	4,394	1,877
Walton	4,587	7,757	1,404	3,725	3,561	5,796
Washington	3,841	2,108	1,510	1,045	2,254	1,165
TOTAL	**1,663,493**	**1,694,838**	**760,474**	**982,405**	**1,534,087**	**917,378**

Unfortunately for the Republicans, if any party momentum had previously existed behind absentee voting, it seemed to have been overshadowed by the rise of early voting in 2008. While the absentee ballot share in Florida's total vote rose sharply from 17.7% in 2004 to 23.1 percent in 2008, the percent of voters who chose to vote early rose even more sharply from 18.6% to 31.5%. The Republican dominance in absentee voting was not enough to offset the disproportionately Democratic turnout at early voting sites. Republicans outvoted Democrats in early voting in only 14 out of 67 counties. In these 14 counties, an average of 16.2% more Republicans than Democrats turned out to vote early. The other 53 counties had a strong early voting turnout of Democrats and showed an average of 34.9% more Democrat early voters than Republicans. The Democrats voted early in a big way. While Republicans narrowly turned out more often on election day and sent in 12.8% more absentee votes, Florida's Democratic voters cast a staggering 25.2% more early votes than did Republicans.

The impact of the Obama campaign's early voting rallies and events across Florida can be seen in the number of ballots cast in each location. In Tampa, where celebrities were recruited to appear and encourage early voting, Democrats turned out a mere 1% more than Republicans on election day and sent in 5% fewer absentee ballots, but they voted early a substantial 33% more often than their Republican counterparts. In Miami-Dade County, which featured early voting marches, the numbers were similar. Democrats turned out slightly more on election day and sent in fewer absentee ballots, but turned out to vote early 36% more than Republicans. In Jacksonville, which was the site of an appearance by Barack Obama himself, Republicans dominated election day votes and absentee votes by 4% and 12% respectively, but Democrats accounted for nearly 65% of early voters in the county.

The example of Jacksonville (Duval County) and its polling numbers convey a common yet surprising theme that was observed in counties across the state during the 2008 election. Fifteen counties in the state reported similar results to those in Duval County, which were characterized by Republican dominance in election day turnout and in absentee voting accompanied by early voting turnout numbers in favor of Democrats. This trend seems to reinforce the assumption that the overwhelmingly Democratic tide of early voting was enough to effect results in even traditionally conservative counties. In fact, of the 14 previously mentioned counties that had higher turnouts of Republicans than Democrats during early voting, 11 posted figures showing at least 20% more Republicans voting on election day than Democrats, and all 14 counties showed Republican election day turnout advantages of at least 9.4%. This seems to suggest that the only counties that were able to retain Republican dominance in early voting were counties that had been historically very conservative. Any county with a Republican turnout advantage margin of 9.3% or less on election day posted numbers showing Democratic superiority in early voting turnout.

THE PATTERN OF RESULTS

In an earlier section of this book, the 2008 election in Florida was described as a reinstating election. For the Democrats it represented the return of their Party to its "rightful" position, given the number of party identifiers it had within the electorate. Although the Democrats have, since the mind of man runneth not back, maintained a majority in both voter registration and in partisan identification in Florida, in the previous 40 years they had rarely won the presidential race. In the 13 presidential elections beginning with 1960, the Democrats had won only 3 times and had averaged only 42% of the two party vote over that time period. In the four presidential elections held between 1976 and 1988, the Republicans averaged 60.3% of the vote and threatened to "realign" Florida and turn the formerly one-party Democratic state into one that was one-party Republican. Table 4.2 shows the results of these elections.

Table 4.2. Presidential Vote Outcomes in Florida (1960–2008)

Year	*Candidates*	*Percentage of Vote*
1960	Nixon/Lodge (REP)*	51.5%
	Kennedy/Johnson (DEM)	48.5%
1964	Goldwater/Miller (REP)	48.8%
	Johnson/Humphrey (DEM)*	51.2%
1968	Nixon/Agnew (REP)*	40.5%
	Humphrey/Muskie (DEM)	30.9%
1972	Nixon/Agnew (REP)*	71.9%
	McGovern/Shriver (DEM)	27.8%
1976	Ford/Dole (REP)	46.6%
	Carter/Mondale (DEM)*	51.9%
1980	Reagan/Bush (REP)*	55.5%
	Carter/Mondale (DEM)	38.5%
1984	Reagan/Bush (REP)*	65.3%
	Mondale/Ferraro (DEM)	34.7%
1988	Bush/Quayle (REP)*	60.9%
	Dukakis/Bentson (DEM)	38.5%
1992	Bush/Quayle (REP)*	40.9%
	Clinton/Gore (DEM)	39.0%
1996	Dole/Kemp (REP)	42.3%
	Clinton/Gore (DEM)*	48.0%
2000	Bush/Cheney (REP)*	48.8%
	Gore/Lieberman (DEM)	48.8%
2004	Bush/Cheney (REP)*	52.1%
	Kerry/Edwards (DEM)	47.1%
2008	McCain/Palin (REP)	48.2%
	Obama/Biden (DEM)*	51.0%

With the adoption of ideas spawned by the Democratic Leadership Council and with Bill Clinton at the top of the Democratic ticket in 1992, the party began to moderate its position on a variety of issues that had led to its definition as too liberal for the South. Subsequently, Florida began to return to its Democratic roots in presidential elections and interparty competition increased substantially. Since 1992, the average margin of victory in Florida, regardless of which party won, has been 3%. The Democrats won two of the five elections held during that time period and virtually tied a third. The Republicans won three, one by fewer than 600 votes. Thus a pattern of highly competitive presidential politics has become the norm in the Sunshine State; it is now a "battleground" state.

THE COUNTY-BY-COUNTY RESULTS

In 1976, Jimmy Carter won the presidential election in Florida by 5.2% of the vote and by achieving voting majorities in 45 of the state's 67 counties. From that point forward until 2008, the base of the Democratic Party crumbled, its presidential candidates were victorious in only one other election (1996) and the number of counties in which it was able to achieve victory dwindled, even though Democratic voter registration continued to be higher than Republican in nearly two-thirds of the counties. In Carter's re-election campaign in1980, the number of counties voting Democratic dropped from 45 to 21 and in both 1984 and 1988 only one county, Gadsen, supported the Party's candidate. In 1996 Bill Clinton became the second Democrat to win Florida since 1964 and voters in 31 counties supported his candidacy, still fewer than half of the state's counties. Since that election, and including 2008, the Party's geographical base has been concentrated in 11 to 15 counties.

Only nine counties supported Democratic presidential candidates in all five of the presidential elections held between 1992 and 2008. They constitute about one third of the registered voters in the state and include the "urbanites" in the four southernmost counties on the East Coast, Palm Beach, Broward, Miami/Dade and Monroe, "ruralites" in four counties in traditional "Old South" North Florida, Alachua, Jefferson, Gadsen and Leon, and Volusia County, located on the Atlantic Coast in North Central Florida. Presidential voting behavior in Florida's counties between 1992 and 2008 is displayed in Figure 4.2.

In 2008, voters in 15 counties supported the candidacy of Barack Obama and those in 52 counties supported John McCain. The 15 included the nine mentioned above and Orange, Hillsborough, St Lucie, Osceola, Pinellas and Flagler. The addition of Osceola, Orange, Hillsborough, and Pinellas represent Democratic campaign success in the "battleground" counties along the I-40 cor-

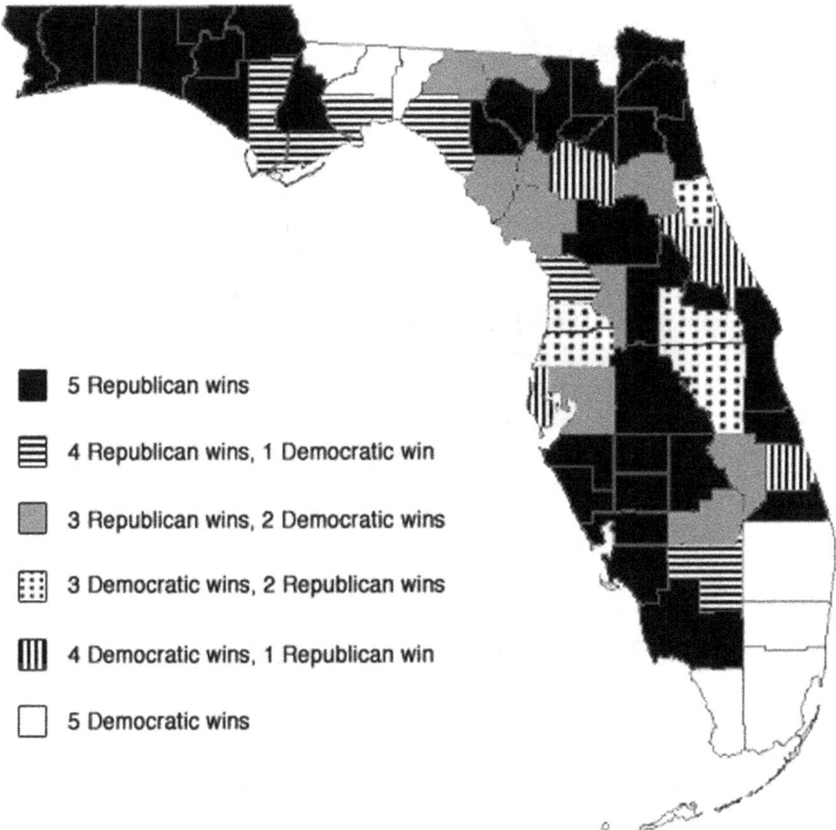

Figure 4.2. Presidential Voting Trends in Florida, 1998–2008.

ridor that stretches from Orlando on the east coast to Tampa/St Petersburg on the west. It is in these counties where most of the state's independent voters reside and their inclusion in the Democratic victory coalition demonstrated some success on the part of Barack Obama in appealing to these crossover voters.

At the same time, population shifts, especially the growth of the non-Cuban Hispanic community in Orange and Osceola counties helped the Democrats immensely. Increases in the Puerto Rican community in Orlando combined with the African American community to produce a 7.3% increase in Democratic Party registration in Orange County between 1996 and 2000 and brought that county into the Democratic fold in the 2000 election for the first time since Harry Truman was the Democratic candidate. Between 2000 and 2008, Democratic registration increased another 65% in Orange and that county has now sided with the Democrats for three presidential elections in a row and appears to be moving to take its place as a reliable part of the

Democratic base vote. At the same time, growth of the non-Cuban Hispanic community in Osceola County helped produced a 19,000 vote victory for Obama in 2008, when John Kerry lost that county by 4,400 votes in 2004.

In general, Obama's victory came by changing the margins which separated John Kerry and George Bush in the 2004 election. Although Obama won only 15 counties, he was able to improve on the Kerry/Bush margin in 41 of the state's 67 counties. In a few (Osceola, Hillsborough) he turned losses into victories. In others (Miami/Dade, Orange) he increased the 2004 margin of victory, but in most he simply turned large losses into smaller ones (Duval, Seminole, Escambia). This was the outcome of Obama's decision to contest the election in all parts of the state and not simply where there were large numbers of Democrats. He employed this strategy at the national level and in Florida. It produced a victory at both levels.

The county distribution of the vote in Florida in 2008 and the changes in the margins of victory/loss between 2004 and 2008 are displayed in Table 4.3.

EXPLAINING INCREASED COMPETITIVENESS

The foregoing analysis suggests that the change in the nature of party competition in recent Florida elections is a function of party messages, candidate appeal and changes in the demographics of the state. National Democrats clearly recognized the need to develop a campaign message that would resonate with a broad segment of the nation's electorate and to put forward candidates who had more general appeal than George McGovern, Michael Dukakis, and Walter Mondale. Such changes were particularly important in southern states such as Florida where the Republican focus on small government, family values and strong defense had tremendous appeal and when the Democrats nominated Jimmy Carter, Bill Clinton, Al Gore, John Kerry and Barack Obama, they began to have greater success in presidential elections, both in the nation and in Florida.

Nevertheless, in Florida, in particular, changes in the nature of the state's population and its electorate were of equal, if not greater, importance to Democratic performance. Between 1988 and 2008, the percentage of eligible voters in the state who are white declined by 8.7% and the percentage of the electorate who were black, Asian and Hispanic all increased. In addition, the composition of the Hispanic population changed and turnout rates for minority voters in the state increased while those for whites decreased. (Pew Research Center) All of these changes benefitted the Democrats at the expense of the Republicans.

Table 4.3. Distribution of Vote by County (2004–2008)

County	2004				2008			
	Bush/Cheney (REP)	Kerry/Edwards (DEM)	Margin (REP)	Margin (DEM)	McCain/Palin (REP)	Obama/Biden (DEM)	Margin (REP)	Margin (DEM)
Alachua	47,762	62,504		13%	48,513	75,565		22%
Baker	7,738	2,180	56%		8,672	2,327	58%	
Bay	53,404	21,068	43%		56,683	23,653	41%	
Bradford	7,557	3,244	40%		8,136	3,430	41%	
Brevard	153,068	110,309	16%		157,589	127,620	11%	
Broward	244,674	453,873		30%	237,729	492,640		35%
Calhoun	3,782	2,116	28%		4,345	1,821	41%	
Charlotte	44,428	34,256	13%		45,205	39,031	7%	
Citrus	39,500	29,277	15%		43,706	31,460	16%	
Clay	62,078	18,971	53%		67,203	26,697	43%	
Collier	83,631	43,392	31%		86,379	54,450	23%	
Columbia	16,758	8,031	35%		18,670	9,171	34%	
DeSoto	5,524	3,913	17%		5,632	4,383	12%	
Dixie	4,434	1,960	39%		5,194	1,925	46%	
Duval	220,190	158,610	16%		210,537	202,618	2%	
Escambia	93,566	48,329	32%		91,411	61,572	20%	
Flagler	19,633	18,578	3%		23,951	24,726		2%
Franklin	3,472	2,401	18%		3,818	2,134	28%	
Gadsden	6,253	14,629		40%	6,811	15,582		39%
Gilchrist	4,936	2,017	42%		5,656	1,996	48%	
Glades	2,443	1,718	17%		1,938	1,381	17%	
Gulf	4,805	2,407	33%		4,980	2,149	40%	

Table 4.3. *(Continued)*

Hamilton	2,792	2,260	11%		3,179	2,364	15%	
Hardee	5,049	2,149	40%		4,763	2,568	30%	
Hendry	5,757	3,960	18%		5,780	4,998	7%	
Hernando	42,635	37,187	7%		45,021	41,886	4%	
Highlands	25,878	15,347	26%		26,221	18,135	18%	
Hillsborough	245,576	214,132	7%		236,355	272,963		7%
Holmes	6,412	1,810	56%		7,033	1,446	66%	
Indian River	36,938	23,956	21%		40,176	29,710	15%	
Jackson	12,122	7,555	23%		13,717	7,671	28%	
Jefferson	3,298	4,135		11%	3,797	4,088		4%
Lafayette	2,460	845	49%		2,679	642	61%	
Lake	74,389	48,221	21%		82,802	62,948	14%	
Lee	144,176	93,860	21%		147,608	119,701	10%	
Leon	51,615	83,873		24%	55,705	91,747		24%
Levy	10,410	6,074	26%		11,754	6,711	27%	
Liberty	1,927	1,070	29%		2,339	895	45%	
Madison	4,191	4,050	2%		4,544	4,270	3%	
Manatee	81,318	61,262	14%		80,721	70,034	7%	
Marion	81,283	57,271	17%		89,628	70,839	12%	
Martin	41,362	30,208	16%		44,143	33,508	14%	
Miami-Dade	361,095	409,732		6%	360,551	499,831		16%
Monroe	19,467	19,654		0.5%	18,933	20,907		5%
Nassau	23,783	8,573	47%		27,403	10,618	44%	
Okaloosa	69,693	19,368	57%		68,789	25,872	45%	
Okeechobee	6,978	5,153	15%		7,561	5,108	19%	
Orange	192,539	193,354		0.2%	186,832	273,009		19%
Osceola	43,117	38,633	5%		40,086	59,962		20%
Palm Beach	212,688	328,687		21%	226,037	361,271		23%

Pasco	103,230	84,749	10%		110,104	102,417	4%	
Pinellas	225,686	225,460	0.1%		210,066	248,299		8%
Polk	123,559	86,009	18%		128,878	113,865	6%	
Putnam	18,311	12,412	19%		19,637	13,236	19%	
Santa Rosa	52,059	14,659	56%		55,972	19,470	48%	
Sarasota	104,692	88,442	8%		102,897	102,686	0.1%	
Seminole	108,172	76,971	17%		105,070	99,335	3%	
St. Johns	59,196	26,399	38%		69,222	35,791	32%	
St. Lucie	47,592	51,835		4%	52,512	67,125		12%
Sumter	19,800	11,534	26%		30,866	17,655	27%	
Suwannee	11,153	4,522	42%		12,534	4,916	44%	
Taylor	5,467	3,049	28%		6,457	2,803	39%	
Union	3,396	1,251	46%		3,940	1,300	50%	
Volusia	111,924	115,519		2%	113,938	127,795		6%
Wakulla	6,777	4,896	16%		8,877	5,311	25%	
Walton	17,555	6,213	48%		19,561	7,174	46%	
Washington	7,369	2,912	43%		8,178	2,863	48%	
Total	**3,964,522**	**3,583,544**	**5%**		**4,045,624**	**4,282,074**		**3%**

African Americans have been reliably and strongly Democratic since the 1960's and an increase in their numbers goes directly to the Democrats bottom line. With an African American at the head of the ticket in 2008, this group was motivated to turn out in record numbers. While most Asians, 35%, do not identify with any political party, more than twice as many of those who do define themselves politically see themselves as Democrats. The totals are 32% to 14%. While the preferences vary among Asian ethnic groups, in the 2008 election, 41% of Asian Americans supported Obama as compared to 24% for McCain. (Junn, Lee, Wong and Ramakrishnan. 2009)

It is the changes in the Hispanic vote that have had the greatest impact on Florida politics. Traditionally, the Cubans have made up the largest share of the Hispanic vote and they have been aggressively Republican. In recent years, non-Cuban Hispanics have come to dominate this segment of the population and they tend to reflect the partisan preferences of Hispanics outside of Florida, namely the Democrats. At the same time the Cuban-Hispanics are slowly changing as the generation of those who left Cuba in 1959 and 1960 in the aftermath of the Castro revolution are being replaced by those who were born and raised in the U.S. come to maturity. This later group is arrayed along a broader spectrum of partisanship than are their parents and grandparents.

The political impact of these changes in the Hispanic population is perhaps best seen in Central Florida, around Orlando. There are now about 659,000 Hispanics in the counties of Brevard, Lake, Orange, Osceola, Polk, Seminole and Volusia. That is about 18 percent of the region's 3.6 million residents. With their movement toward the Democrats, what were formerly seen as "battleground" counties may become safer for one of the two parties.

Part II

VOTING BEHAVIOR IN THE FLORIDA PRESIDENTIAL ELECTION

Chapter Five

Who Voted and in What Numbers?

As the 2008 election moved to its close, political pundits around the nation began to forecast an unusually large turnout of voters, driven largely by the energy surrounding the candidacy of Barack Obama. As a historic figure in American politics, he generated great emotion and spurred new interest in politics within some segments of the American public. This chapter asks whether or not this heightened interest affected voter participation in Florida. The question is addressed through an examination of both voter registration and turnout in the election and by a comparison of the 2008 figures to those in other presidential elections, both in Florida and in the nation.

The analysis begins with a description of changes in voter registration in the state and then looks at the way in which the voter turnout rate in the 2008 election compared to that in other years. A voter turnout rate is the total number of votes cast divided by some base number of people. The base can be defined as the voting age population (VAP), the voter eligible population (VEP) or the number of persons registered to vote. Political scientists argue that the VEP is the more accurate measure of turnout because it omits persons who are ineligible to vote, such as noncitizens, felons and the mentally incompetent. (McDonald and Popkin. 2001) Nevertheless, both the VAP and the VEP provide comparable measures of turnout across states and therefore permit cross state and over time analyzes. Using voter registration as the denominator is problematic because of the unreliability of voter registration figures. The VAP and the VEP are included in this analysis.

VOTER REGISTRATION AND TURNOUT IN FLORIDA IN HISTORICAL PERSPECTIVE

Over the years Floridians have been more reluctant to register and to vote than have citizens in most other states in the nation. Table 5.1 shows that in the seven presidential elections between 1976 and 2000, an average of 69% of the citizens of voting age in Florida were registered to vote. This average ranks about 33rd in the nation. In these same elections, an average of only 44.6% of the voting age population actually turned out to vote and during that time period the voter turnout rate in Florida never surpassed the average turnout in the nation; it ranked about 41st in the nation. Turnout among Democrats and Republicans has been even lower than the overall rate. Over the time period 1968 to 2008, Democratic turnout has averaged 22.3% and Republican turnout has been 27.7%. (Data from the U.S. Elections Project at George Mason University and from the Center for the Study of the American Electorate.)

The 2000 presidential election in Florida changed the state's lackadaisical behavior toward its electoral system. In the aftermath of the extraordinarily close race between Al Gore and George Bush, the state made changes to its voting technology and both of the major political parties redoubled their efforts to register their supporters and to mobilize them at election time. These efforts produced substantial improvement in both registration and turnout. (See Tables 5.1 & 5.3for registration data)The number of persons registered to vote increased by 28.5% between 2000 and 2008 and voter turnout increased by 17% during this same time period. These two elections became the first in Florida history in which the average voter turnout in the state outstripped the average turnout in the nation. Using VAP data, voter turnout in 2004 in Florida was 62.7% as compared to 60.5% nationally. In 2008 the comparable figures were 62.4% and 60.7%. Using VEP data, the turnout in 2004 was 60.9% for the nation and 66.2% in Florida. In 2008 the comparable figures were 61.7% and 67.5%.

VOTER REGISTRATION IN THE 2008 ELECTION

In the aftermath of the 2000 presidential election, both major political parties engaged in substantial voter registration efforts and both produced substantial increases in their parties' voter rolls. Between 2000 and 2004, overall registration in Florida increased by 17.6% and over one and one half million new voters were added to the voter rolls. The Democrats increased voter registration by 12.0% and the Republicans increased by 13.4%. The registration

Table 5.1. Voter Registration in Florida and the Nation (1968–2008)

Year	1968	1972	1976	1980	1984	1988	1992	1996	2000	2004	2008
National Registration %	74.3	72.3	66.7	66.9	68.3	66.6	68.2	65.9	63.9	65.9	64.9
Florida's Registration %	N/A	68.7	62.7	69.6	69.5	70.3	71.4	68.8	69.9	71.7	70.4
Florida's Rank	N/A	12*	19*	35	42	30	38	38	27	32	33

activities of the two major political parties may also have had some spillover effect as registration among "Other" parties also went up and dramatically so, by 41.3%. When the 2004 voter registration books were closed the Democrats held a 368,000 person edge in registered voters and claimed 41.2% of the registered voters as adherents. Table 5.2 shows thirty eight per cent (37.7%) of these voters identified with the Republicans, and Independents and members of other parties accounted for 20.9%. Democrats claimed the majority of registered voters in 40 counties and Republicans in 27.

It was against this backdrop that the 2008 presidential candidates began their voter registration efforts in Florida. The Obama campaign was particularly visible and aggressive. Obama himself had a background in voter registration and when he was a community organizer in Chicago in 1992 had led a drive that "altered Chicago's electoral landscape" (Reynolds. 1993. January.) and drove home to him the importance of this activity. Thus he "stressed voter registration from the outset of his campaign, seeing younger or disaffected Americans as a crucial pool of support." (MacGillis and Crites. 2008. October 6.) His voter registration campaign was well financed and attracted highly motivated volunteers.

The Obama campaign employed the full range of voter registration activities. It held "massive, unprecedented" registration efforts on college campuses and held a number of rallies with celebrities such as Miami Heat basketball star Alonso Mourning and Sex and the City actress Cynthia Nixon. Hip-hop stars Jay Z and Wyclef Jean gave free concerts at the Bayfront Park Theater in Miami for those who registered to vote and gave contact information from those who attended to the Obama campaign. In addition, his sizeable field staff canvassed relentlessly through the state employing a variety of technological innovations that included a Web site where voters could request an absentee ballot or find their polling place. While most of his registration

Table 5.2. Voter Registration in Florida by Party Affiliation (1972–2008)

Year	Republicans	Democrats	Other	Total
1972	984,999	2,394,604	117,855	3,497,458
1976	1,138,751	2,750,723	204,834	4,094,000
1980	1,429,645	3,087,427	292,649	4,809,721
1984	1,895,937	3,313,073	365,462	5,574,472
1988	2,360,434	3,264,105	422,808	6,047,347
1992	2,672,968	3,318,565	550,292	6,541,825
1996	3,317,501	3,740,351	1,050,419	8,108,271
2000	3,474,438	3,853,524	1,552,434	8,880,396
2004	3,954,492	4,322,376	2,199,569	10,476,437
2008	4,106,743	4,800,890	2,504,290	11,411,923

activities were basic "Campaigning 101," Obama's money allowed him to utilize these activities on an unprecedented scale. Steve Schale, the Obama state director said "we are absolutely serious about competing for the votes of every single Floridian." (Bender. 2008. Oct 4.) At an estimated cost of $14 dollars to sign up each new voter, the Obama campaign may have spent about $2 million on registrations in Florida.

Complementing these efforts were organizations that registered thousands of voters on their own, such as Project Vote, ACORN, a nationwide group of community organizations, and Women's Voices Women Vote which targets unmarried women. Project Vote and ACORN conducted a joint registration drive and claimed to have signed up 145,000 Floridians. While both organizations profess to be independent, they target voters who are more likely to vote Democratic rather than Republican; minorities, younger voters and less affluent citizens. Indeed, ACORN became the target of multiple complaints from Republicans around the nation about the legality of its registration efforts.

The McCain campaign mounted a less substantial voter registration effort. As has been the case with Republicans for years, it relied upon a large cadre of party volunteers to conduct door-to-door and telephone registration efforts.

As a product of the activities described above, voter registration in Florida increased from 10.4 million in 2004 to 11.4 million in 2008 and 935,486 voters were added to the rolls. Democrats added 478,514 new registrants, Republicans 152,251 and Independents and small "third" parties added 305,000. While this total was a 8.9% increase over 2004, it was substantially smaller than the increase that had taken place between 2000 and 2004. Democrats increased their registration by 11.0% while the Republicans increased by 3.8% and when voter registration closed in October, 2008 Democrat voter registration outnumbered that of Republicans by 694,147. Once again, Independents and other parties increased by a larger percentage than did either major political party, 13.8%.When the voter registration rolls were closed on October 6, 2008, the Democrats had increased slightly and the Republicans had decreased as a percentage of the total registered voters in the state. Democrats constituted 42.0% of the registered voters (up from 41.2% in 2004), Republicans made up 35.9% (down from 37.7%) and Independents and members of other parties represented 21.9%, increasing by 4% their share of the electorate's allegiance and increasing this group's importance in Florida politics.

Between 2004 and 2008, registration increased in all but 4 of the state's 67 counties. Table 5.3 shows that only Broward, Gulf, Hendry and Monroe showed decreases. Nevertheless, the two major parties did not share equally in this overall improvement; the Republicans increased their numbers in 62 of the 67 counties while the Democrats improved in 47. The Democrats decreased in 15 counties and remained stagnant in 4 counties.

Table 5.3. Voter Registration in Florida by County (2004–2008)

	2004			*2008*			*Percent Change*		
County	REP	DEM	Total Registration	REP	DEM	Total Registration	REP	DEM	Total Registration
Alachua	39,605	71,948	142,358	42,476	80,686	154,706	+7.2%	+12.1%	+8.7%
Baker	3,126	8,926	12,887	5,188	7,896	14,172	+66.0%	–11.5%	+10.0%
Bay	44,751	39,707	101,315	52,028	39,321	110,739	+16.3%	–1.0%	+9.3%
Bradford	4,168	9,039	14,721	5,588	8,424	15,732	+34.1%	–6.8%	+6.9%
Brevard	151,535	123,578	338,195	152,836	130,953	351,488	+0.9%	+6.0%	+3.9%
Broward	283,736	533,976	1,058,069	243,743	533,409	1,008,656	–14.1%	–0.1%	–4.7%
Calhoun	993	6,879	8,350	1,371	6,694	8,622	+38.1%	–2.7%	+3.3%
Charlotte	51,110	36,306	113,808	51,404	38,564	118,837	+0.6%	+6.2%	+4.4%
Citrus	37,653	35,340	90,780	42,845	37,786	102,742	+13.8%	+6.9%	+13.2%
Clay	60,192	27,282	106,464	67,173	31,468	120,656	+11.6%	+15.3%	+13.3%
Collier	89,559	41,082	168,673	101,848	52,586	203,075	+13.7%	+28.0%	+20.4%
Columbia	10,737	19,374	34,282	13,510	19,606	38,272	+25.8%	+1.2%	+11.6%
DeSoto	3,787	8,836	14,901	4,192	8,900	15,613	+10.7%	+0.7%	+4.8%
Dixie	1,454	7,495	9,676	2,181	7,456	10,775	+50.0%	–0.5%	+11.4%
Duval	190,111	238,264	515,202	196,069	244,707	536,588	+3.1%	+2.7%	+4.2%
Escambia	83,165	77,250	189,833	84,777	78,694	195,193	+1.9%	+1.9%	+2.8%
Flagler	19,179	17,940	47,068	22,212	22,896	60,079	+15.8%	+27.6%	+27.6%
Franklin	1,212	5,893	7,620	1,473	5,670	7,722	+21.5%	–3.8%	+1.3%
Gadsden	3,012	22,280	26,884	3,859	24,171	30,128	+28.1%	+8.5%	+12.1%
Gilchrist	2,750	5,295	9,035	3,987	5,392	10,721	+45.0%	+1.8%	+18.7%
Glades	1,479	3,867	5,963	1,813	3,896	6,584	+22.6%	+0.7%	+10.4%
Gulf	2,557	6,464	9,627	2,831	5,628	9,123	+10.7%	–12.9%	–5.2%
Hamilton	1,140	6,029	7,645	1,394	5,636	7,688	+22.3%	–6.5%	+0.6%
Hardee	2,779	6,630	10,399	3,716	6,723	11,802	+33.7%	+1.4%	+13.5%
Hendry	5,279	9,688	17,144	5,419	9,203	16,936	+2.7%	–5.0%	–1.2%
Hernando	45,266	42,554	109,656	49,093	47,891	123,013	+8.5%	+12.5%	+12.2%
Highlands	26,752	23,939	60,176	28,671	26,383	66,092	+7.2%	+10.2%	+9.8%
Hillsborough	217,766	258,882	621,201	233,235	300,896	701,464	+7.1%	+16.2%	+12.9%
Holmes	2,344	7,986	10,982	3,209	7,416	11,513	+36.9%	–7.1%	+4.8%
Indian River	41,866	24,515	81,643	43,947	27,871	90,053	+5.0%	+13.7%	+10.3%
Jackson	5,962	19,411	27,138	7,018	19,121	28,128	+17.7%	–1.5%	+3.6%

Jefferson	1,929	6,726	9,300	2,207	7,269	10,310	+14.4%	+8.1%	+10.9%
Lafayette	570	3,570	4,309	899	3,338	4,469	+57.7%	--6.5%	+3.7%
Lake	76,387	55,258	161,259	84,570	66,345	188,702	+10.7%	+20.1%	+17.0%
Lee	144,948	90,716	304,937	147,241	99,413	320,512	+1.6%	+9.6%	+5.1%
Leon	45,578	97,672	171,182	47,221	100,399	174,544	+3.6%	+2.8%	+2.0%
Levy	6,241	13,503	22,617	7,929	14,070	25,924	+27.0%	+4.2%	+14.6%
Liberty	320	3,597	4,075	332	3,804	4,304	+3.8%	+5.8%	+5.6%
Madison	1,695	9,042	11,371	2,211	9,133	12,278	+30.4%	+1.0%	+8.0%
Manatee	84,804	63,305	191,635	88,620	69,503	206,211	+4.5%	+9.8%	+7.6%
Marion	79,572	73,168	184,257	89,436	85,426	214,722	+12.4%	+16.8%	+16.5%
Martin	51,869	27,203	98,857	50,457	29,265	101,155	--2.7%	+7.6%	+2.3%
Miami-Dade	368,334	453,631	1,058,801	382,286	554,001	1,243,315	+3.8%	+22.1%	+17.4%
Monroe	19,874	18,563	51,377	18,950	18,128	50,136	--4.6%	--2.3%	--2.4%
Nassau	20,300	15,218	41,353	24,772	15,583	47,501	+22.0%	+2.4%	+14.9%
Okaloosa	72,885	31,526	127,455	74,850	31,052	129,373	+2.7%	--1.5%	+1.5%
Okeechobee	5,537	10,891	18,627	6,050	10,276	18,859	+9.3%	--5.6%	+1.2%
Orange	186,614	213,702	531,774	189,658	267,031	604,243	+1.6%	+25.0%	+13.6%
Osceola	42,462	52,064	129,487	40,486	59,652	136,544	--4.7%	+14.6%	+5.4%
Palm Beach	233,495	329,232	729,575	246,600	381,814	831,423	+5.6%	+16.0%	+14.0%
Pasco	106,649	99,272	265,974	114,954	109,767	294,431	+7.8%	+10.6%	+10.7%
Pinellas	231,652	223,544	590,989	237,749	249,454	643,423	+2.6%	+11.6%	+8.9%
Polk	115,211	125,870	295,742	124,269	140,220	332,015	+7.9%	+11.4%	+12.3%
Putnam	12,728	26,184	45,344	13,775	25,755	46,432	+8.2%	--1.6%	+2.4%
Santa Rosa	53,853	27,083	96,359	60,721	28,279	107,253	+12.8%	+4.4%	+11.3%
Sarasota	115,317	74,986	240,592	117,603	85,382	260,618	+2.0%	+13.9%	+8.3%
Seminole	107,613	77,964	241,230	107,516	89,956	259,336	--0.1%	+15.4%	+7.5%
St. Johns	58,436	31,051	109,635	69,596	36,341	131,744	+19.1%	+17.0%	+20.2%
St. Lucie	50,436	57,128	137,951	52,250	70,065	157,676	+3.6%	+22.6%	+14.3%
Sumter	17,631	16,553	40,523	27,973	21,361	59,913	+58.7%	+29.0%	+47.8%
Suwannee	5,885	13,941	21,930	7,623	14,372	24,791	+29.5%	+3.1%	+13.0%
Taylor	2,170	8,679	11,481	2,971	9,179	13,088	+36.9%	+5.8%	+14.0%
Union	1,291	5,331	7,063	1,958	4,803	7,273	+51.7%	--9.9%	+3.0%
Volusia	111,372	126,405	309,930	111,577	133,468	326,854	+0.2%	+5.6%	+5.5%
Wakulla	3,730	10,293	15,396	5,213	11,231	18,565	+39.8%	+9.1%	+20.6%
Walton	16,413	12,051	32,777	19,602	11,678	36,847	+19.4%	--3.1%	+12.4%
Washington	3,666	9,668	14,421	5,070	9,320	15,938	+38.3%	--3.6%	+10.5%
Total	**3,892,492**	**4,261,249**	**10,301,290**	**4,064,301**	**4,722,076**	**11,247,634**	**+4.4%**	**+10.8%**	**+9.2%**

Most of the decline for the Democrats (12 of the 15 counties involved) came in the traditional Southern oriented counties of North Florida where racial bias lingers over the landscape and where Democrats had been voting for Republican candidates for years. In these 12 counties, Republican registration increased by an average of 31.3% and Democratic registration *declined* by an average of 4.9%. It appears that in 2008, the candidacy of Barack Obama pushed some Democrats formally out of the Party.

Only two counties changed their registration allegiance from one party to the other in 2008 and both went from a majority of Republicans to a majority of Democrats. In Flagler county, the Democrats went from a 561 voter deficit to a 684 majority and in Pinellas they went from 8,108 down to 11,705 up. Most of the increases for Democrats came from 4 counties; Miami/Dade where they increased their totals by over 100,000 registrants, Orange and Palm Beach where they gained more than 50,000 new adherents each and Hillsborough with 42,000 new registered Democrats. Large gains for the Republicans came in Collier County (13.7% increase), Lake County (10.7%) and Hernando County (8.4%). When the Florida Division of Elections closed its books on October 6, 2008, 42 counties had a majority of Democrats and 25 had a majority of Republicans.

Slightly more than one third of the increase in voter registration between 2004 and 2008 came from the state's largest minority populations, African Americans and Hispanics. African Americans who make up about 16% of the state's population and about 12% of the electorate constituted nearly 19% of the new registrations. Hispanics, who also constitute about 12% of the registered voters, made up about 20% of the newly registered, almost the same as their share of the state's population. (MacGillis. 2008. Oct. 7) When the voter rolls were closed on October 6, there were 1,468,682 African Americans registered to vote and 1,355,270 Hispanics.

Not surprisingly, the African American registrants were overwhelmingly Democratic. Eighty three percent (83.6%) were registered with that party, 12.1% were registered as Independents or other parties and only 4.2% were registered Republican. More interestingly, and more importantly from a political standpoint, is the partisan breakdown among Hispanic voters. As suggested earlier, Florida's Hispanics have for years been the most Republican-leaning in the nation because the Cubans, who were strong supporters of that Party, were nearly 70% of that population. More recently, increases in Florida's Hispanic population have come from Puerto Rico, Mexico and Central America and these populations, particularly the Puerto Ricans, are more inclined toward the Democrats. The priorities of these voters are jobs, the economy, and education. They don't care about Fidel Castro and exhibit some resentment over U.S. policy that gives Cuban immigrants preferential treatment. In 2008, 37.8% of the Hispanic population was registered with the Democrats, 32.8% with the Republicans and 29.4% as Independents or other parties.

The increase in Hispanic registrations can be attributed to the two presidential campaigns' efforts to engage this community and also to a number of organizations that registered voters independently of the political parties, including *Democracia USA* which registered 138,000 Hispanics voters nationwide and concentrated on Florida, Philadelphia, New Jersey and other areas with high concentrations of Hispanic citizens.

As voter registration came to a close in Florida in 2008, a new partisan balance was seen in the state. The Democrats, always the majority party, had increased its 2004 lead over the Republicans by about 289,000 registered voters, solidified its lead among African Americans and taken the lead among Hispanic voters. At the same time, Independents and a variety of "third" parties also made substantial gains in the state, ensuring that future campaigns will continue to be highly competitive.

VOTER TURNOUT IN THE 2008 ELECTION

Despite aggressive voter registration and get-out-the vote efforts on the part of both the major political parties in Florida, the turnout in the 2008 presidential election was only slightly different from that in 2004. It was certainly not the "tsunami" some prognosticators had predicted. Both of the measures of voter turnout showed only small changes. Measured as a percentage of the voting age population, or VAP, voter turnout actually decreased, by 3/10ths of one percent. At the same time, the voting eligible population (VEP) data showed a 1.3% increase. Despite these narrow percentage changes, more people voted for President in Florida in 2008 than had ever done so before, a total of 8,390,744. In addition, Barack Obama garnered the largest number of votes ever awarded to a presidential candidate in the state, 4,722,076.

TURNOUT ACROSS COUNTIES

As might be suspected, turnout, shown in table 5.4, varied across the 67 counties of the state. The turnout, measured as the percentage of the voting age population, was lowest in DeSoto (38.8%), Hardee (35.5%), and Hendry (38.8%). It was highest in Sumter (79.0%), in St. Johns (73.9%), and in Leon (71.1%).

Table 5.4. Voter Turnout in Florida by County (2004–2008)

	2004		*2008*	
County	**Turnout**	**% Turnout**	**Turnout**	**% Turnout**
Alachua	111,566	62.4%	126,322	64.3%
Baker	10,048	56.8%	11,156	56.6%
Bay	75,234	62.4%	81,692	64.6%
Bradford	10,917	50.0%	11,777	50.8%
Brevard	266,160	65.0%	289,931	67.4%
Broward	709,724	53.6%	739,873	55.0%
Calhoun	6,008	58.7%	6,317	58.3%
Charlotte	80,196	60.7%	86,035	68.4%
Citrus	69,701	64.2%	76,865	64.9%
Clay	81,731	66.9%	94,814	67.7%
Collier	129,231	55.1%	143,120	57.0%
Columbia	25,082	53.7%	28,360	53.0%
DeSoto	9,549	35.4%	10,211	38.8%
Dixie	6,474	57.5%	7,377	61.5%
Duval	382,006	63.5%	417,666	66.0%
Escambia	143,849	62.9%	155,506	66.1%
Flagler	38,557	67.9%	49,356	66.4%
Franklin	5,974	73.8%	6,130	66.3%
Gadsden	21,094	61.8%	22,628	62.6%
Gilchrist	7,050	57.2%	7,870	58.2%
Glades	4,204	47.4%	4,293	46.3%
Gulf	7,320	66.4%	7,284	55.5%
Hamilton	5,131	46.6%	5,651	49.9%

Table 5.4. *(Continued)*

Hardee	7,284	35.9%	7,476	35.5%
Hendry	9,818	36.8%	10,976	38.8%
Hernando	80,764	66.4%	88,624	63.7%
Highlands	41,876	55.7%	45,404	55.6%
Hillsborough	464,849	56.8%	515,983	58.9%
Holmes	8,351	56.5%	8,719	57.2%
Indian River	61,707	61.4%	71,145	66.5%
Jackson	19,908	53.3%	21,783	55.0%
Jefferson	7,502	65.0%	8,017	67.7%
Lafayette	3,352	56.6%	3,416	53.1%
Lake	124,488	59.8%	148,144	59.9%
Lee	241,663	59.1%	271,772	57.8%
Leon	136,638	71.3%	149,319	71.1%
Levy	16,742	58.3%	18,883	61.1%
Liberty	3,051	51.9%	3,337	52.8%
Madison	8,345	57.4%	8,959	60.9%
Manatee	143,983	62.0%	152,924	61.4%
Marion	140,354	61.0%	163,297	61.9%
Martin	72,736	64.9%	79,005	69.6%
Miami-Dade	778,953	43.9%	872,260	46.8%
Monroe	39,629	61.1%	40,690	66.7%
Nassau	32,827	67.9%	38,570	70.7%
Okaloosa	89,957	65.8%	96,042	70.0%
Okeechobee	12,249	41.9%	12,903	42.4%
Orange	390,706	53.3%	466,002	57.9%
Osceola	82,204	50.9%	100,925	51.6%
Palm Beach	547,340	56.3%	594,854	59.4%
Pasco	191,909	59.5%	217,115	58.4%

(continued)

Table 5.4. *(Continued)*

Pinellas	457,581	61.5%	468,700	63.4%
Polk	211,399	53.5%	246,538	55.9%
Putnam	31,072	56.8%	33,393	59.3%
Santa Rosa	67,498	64.6%	76,583	66.1%
Sarasota	196,413	66.4%	208,683	66.9%
Seminole	186,617	63.2%	206,970	65.0%
St. Johns	86,631	72.5%	106,427	73.9%
St. Lucie	100,374	56.9%	121,598	59.2%
Sumter	32,005	63.0%	49,244	79.0%
Suwannee	15,879	54.7%	17,811	57.5%
Taylor	8,614	58.5%	9,449	54.6%
Union	4,714	40.0%	5,359	43.0%
Volusia	229,193	60.1%	245,842	61.3%
Wakulla	11,820	56.3%	14,444	58.7%
Walton	24,065	63.1%	27,238	64.0%
Washington	10,453	61.1%	11,272	59.5%
Total	**7,640,319**	**57.0%**	**8,456,329**	**59.0%**

In general, turnout was higher in counties in which the Republicans were in the majority than in those where the Democrats were the majority party. The turnout in Republican counties averaged 65.2% as opposed to 56.2% in the Democratic counties. Florida Republicans have long argued that they have a get-out-the vote operation that is superior to that of the Democrats and cite the 2008 election as verification. However, Republicans are more likely than Democrats to be characterized by the social and demographic features associated with both registration and voting and it is these characteristics in addition to Party mobilization activities that produce higher levels of voting turnout on the part of Republicans.

Most of the changes between 2004 and 2008 in voter turnout within the counties were, with a few exceptions, quite small. The only double digit changes came in Sumter County (+16.0%) and in Gulf County (-10.9%). The smallest changes were in Highlands County (-.1%) and in Lake County (-.1%).

Chapter Six

Social Groups and the Vote

The analysis to this point has focused on aggregate vote and voter turnout totals. The analysis that follows examines the electoral behavior of specific groups within the electorate. While votes are cast by individuals, group membership influences individual voting behavior and an examination of the behavior of these groups helps to explain the pattern and trends in elections. As group loyalties form and break up, candidate and party fortunes wax and wane. This chapter examines the voting patterns of a variety of social groups and compares their behavior to that of similar groups both in Florida and at the national level in the 2000 and the 2004 elections. This analysis will provide insight into the changing nature of political coalitions both in Florida and in the United States and help explain why Barack Obama won the election. The data for the analysis is displayed in Table 6.1 and is taken from exit polls conducted by MSMBC in the aftermath of the 2004 and 2008 elections.

GROUP VOTING IN FLORIDA: 2004 AND 2008

Floridians responded to Barack Obama's call for a return to the political center and he found widespread support within the electorate. His vote totals in 65% of the social groups employed in this analysis were either equal to or superior to those of John McCain. The groups involved were various categories of gender, age, race, income, Religion, level of education, partisan identification and ideology.

All candidates conduct their campaigns in light of the previous race for their particular office. Candidates representing the party that lost the previous election seek to improve on that performance, while winning party candidates attempt to replicate their party's prior performance. In seeking to improve on previous levels of support for their parties, John McCain and Barack Obama were presented with two possibilities: 1) improve support vis-à-vis their parties' 2004 candidate in particular groups, and/or 2) increase the size of a supportive group relative to the total voting population. As befits a candidate of the party which lost Florida in 2004, but won in 2008, Barack Obama did both. That is, he generated a larger share of the vote than did John Kerry from almost all social groups and he also motivated some groups who supported him to turn out in larger numbers than they had for Kerry.

Obama received a higher level of support than did John Kerry in all but seven of the 41 social group categories for which comparative data are available. In four of these groups the increase was large enough to shift overall support from George Bush to Barack Obama. And finally, while swinging their support from Bush to himself, Obama also boosted substantially the turnout among several groups, including the "baby boomers" (ages 45–64) who went from about one in four Florida voters in 2004 to about one in three in 2008.

Changing Margin Share in Groups

Barack Obama got a larger share of the vote than did John Kerry from 34 of the 41 social groups for which we have data. Table 6.1 shows these data. Only white protestants, white evangelical protestants, individuals whose family incomes were between $50,000 and $74,900 and between $100,000 and $149,000, individuals whose age was 65 or higher, Republicans, and Independents were more supportive of John McCain than Barack Obama. Obama's improved margins over those of John Kerry ranged from 1% among white people to 33% among individuals who did not complete high school. In addition to the group that did not complete high school, Obama also had large increases from Hispanics (27%), Liberals (20%), those with graduate educations (25%), those whose family income exceeded $200,000 (21%) and those between the ages 45–64 (20%). In addition, African Americans, who traditionally vote at high levels for Democrats increased their level of support for Obama by 10% over that for Kerry.

John McCain gained more support than George Bush in only one group, Independents, while matching Bush's support in one other group, white Protestants. No group shifted its support from the Democrat's Kerry in 2004 to the Republican's McCain in 2008.

Groups in Florida that supported Obama at exceptionally high levels included African Americans (96%), liberals (91%), Democrats (87%), individuals

Table 6.1. Social Groups and the Presidential Vote in Florida (2004–2008)

	2008				2004					
	McCain	Obama	Margin	Total	Bush	Kerry	Margin	Total	Margin Change	% Dem. Change
Gender										
Male	47	51	4	47	53	46	-7	46	11	5.58%
Female	47	52	5	53	50	49	-1	54	6	3.03%
Age										
18-29	37	61	24	15	41	58	17	17	7	3.66%
30-44	49	49	0	25	53	46	-7	27	7	3.54%
45-64	47	52	5	37	57	42	-15	28	20	10.10%
65+	53	45	-8	22	52	47	-5	27	-3	-1.56%
Race										
White	56	42	-14	71	57	42	-15	71	1	0.43%
Black	4	96	92	13	13	86	73	13	19	9.13%
Hispanic	42	57	15	14	56	44	-12	14	27	13.58%
Party										
Democrat	12	87	75	37	14	85	71	37	4	2.02%
Republican	87	12	-75	34	93	7	-86	41	11	5.12%
Independent	45	52	7	29	41	57	16	23	-9	-4.56%
Ideology										
Liberal	8	91	83	19	18	81	63	20	20	10.10%
Moderate	41	57	16	47	43	56	13	47	3	1.60%
Conservative	77	21	-56	35	86	13	-73	34	17	8.30%
Last Grade of School Completed										
Did not complete high school	29	70	41	3	45	53	8	3	33	16.63%
High School Graduate	41	58	17	20	48	51	3	20	14	7.07%
Some college or associate degree	49	49	0	32	51	48	-3	34	3	1.52%
College Graduate	53	45	-8	32	56	44	-12	27	4	1.92%
Postgraduate Study	41	58	17	13	53	45	-8	15	25	12.67%
Religion										
Protestant	55	43	-12	52	59	40	-19		7	3.47%
White Protestant	68	30	-38	38	68	32	-36		-2	-1.39%

White Evangelical Protestant	81	18	-63	22	95	5	-90		27	13.18%
White Protestant, Not Evangelical	53	45	-8	17			0		-8	
Black Protestant	5	94	89	9			0		89	
Catholic	49	50	1	28	57	42	-15		16	8.08%
White Catholic	53	46	-7	19	59	40	-19		12	6.06%
Hispanic Catholic	43	56	13	8			0		13	
Jewish	x	x	0	4	20	80	60		-60	
Other	18	80	62	6	29	69	40		22	11.22%
None	26	71	45	10	31	66	35		10	5.15%
New Voter										
Yes	40	59	19	12	43	56	13		6	3.03%
No	48	50	2	88	53	46	-7		9	4.56%
Family Income, Previous Year										
Under $15,000	33	66	33	8	40	59	19	9	14	11.74%
$15,000-$29,999	37	62	25	12	39	59	20	15	5	2.42%
$30,000-$49,999	39	59	20	19	48	51	3	22	17	-13.56%
$50,000-$74,999	52	47	-5	23	54	45	-9	21	4	2.02%
$75,000-$99,999	58	39	-19	14	62	37	-25	14	6	2.83%
$100,000-$149,999	58	40	-18	12	56	44	-12	10	-6	-3.18%
$150,000-$199,999	54	45	-9	7	60	38	-22	4	13	6.68%
$200,000 or More	48	51	3	5	59	41	-18	5	21	10.52%

who indicated that their religious affiliation was something "other" than those provided by the interviewer (80%), those who professed to have no religious affiliation (71%)and those who did not complete high school (70%). Those who supported McCain at high levels were Republicans (87%), Conservatives (77%) and white evangelical Protestants (81%).

Twelve percent (12%) of the Florida electorate in 2008 voted for the first time and 59% of them voted for Obama, a 19 point edge within this group. While the percentage of the new voters who voted for Obama was not as great as those in the groups described in the preceding paragraph, it is important. Voting for a candidate of a particular political party for the first time is somewhat like choosing to support the University of North Carolina's basketball team rather than that of Duke University. Once you become loyal to one, you usually stay loyal for some time.

Reversing Group Support

Several of the groups who increased their support for Obama did so at a level that changed the 2004 partisan direction of the group. These included both women and men, Hispanics and the baby boomers whose ages were between 45 and 64.

In 2004 in Florida, George Bush received more votes from both men (53%–46%) and women (50%–49%) than did John Kerry. This represented something of an anomaly since men have regularly supported Republicans at higher levels than Democrats but women have not and a "gender gap" has emerged in which women have been consistently more supportive of Democrats. Nationally, the average gender gap for all presidential elections from 1980 to 2000 was 7% and in the 2000 race, Al Gore got the support of 53% of the women in Florida as opposed to 46% of the men. In 2008 Obama reversed the 2004 anomaly and created something of one himself by winning 51% of men's votes and 52% of women. After all the concern among Democrats that PUMAs and other embittered Hillary Clinton supporters might back John McCain out of spite, women left George Bush and rallied to the support of Barack Obama at only slightly lower levels than they had for Al Gore in 2000. At the national level 84% of those who said they had voted for Clinton during the primaries voted for Obama in the general election.

Two other Florida groups changed allegiance from Republican to Democrat in the 2008 election and there is a good argument to be made that it was the switch in this support that produced the Obama victory. The two groups were Florida's Hispanics and the state's aging "baby-boomers."

In 2004, Hispanics in Florida had supported George Bush over John Kerry by 56% to 44%, and a key objective for John McCain was to retain this support. He failed to do so, and in 2008 this group supported Barack Obama by a margin of 57% to 42%, a 27 point increase and a 13.5% Democratic change from the previous election. The loss of votes by the Republicans in the Hispanic community in Florida was a significant event in the 2008 election and one that carries long-term implications for that Party.

Finally, the baby boomer generation in Florida (ages 45–64) may have swung the election to Barack Obama. Not only did this group shift its support from Bush to Obama by 20 points—one of the largest swings in 2008—it also accounted for the largest increase in voter turnout in the state. In 2004 approximately one in four or about 28% of Florida's voters were aged 45–64; in 2008, about 37%, or one in three voters were baby boomers.

The youth vote (ages 18–24) has been given credit for much of Obama's electoral success both in Florida and the nation, and in Florida Obama did increase his support in this group by 3% over that of John Kerry. However, turnout in this group declined by 2% between 2004 and 2008 and left Obama with only a 3.6% improvement in Democratic support. The 45–64 age group was far more important in Florida, producing a 10.1% change in Democratic support.

Increasing Vote Share

Three segments of the Florida electorate increased their share of the vote by 5% or more between 2004 and 2008. These included age groups 45–64, Independents, and college graduates. One of these, the Independents, supported McCain. The other two supported Obama.

Independents as a percentage of the total vote in Florida increased by 6% between 2004 and 2008. When compared to John Kerry, Obama lost 5% of the vote among this group, creating a -9 point margin change for Obama and a -4.5% Democratic change from the 2004 election. Obama did gain 7% among Republicans as compared to Kerry; an 11 point margin change. And even though Republicans lost 7% of vote share between 2004 and 2008, Obama gained a 5 point margin share and a 5.1% change in this group, somewhat offsetting the loss among Independents.

Obama also gained ground over Kerry and cut his losses among college graduates, who had increased their share of the vote from 27% to 32%. In 2004, John Kerry lost this group by 12 points. In 2008, Obama lost it by 8 points. Finally, as shown above, Obama profited enormously from the increased turnout of the age group 45–64, which offset the loss of support in the age group 65+, whose share of the vote declined by 5 points.

GROUP VOTING: FLORIDA AND THE NATION

As a contestant for a nationwide office, a presidential candidate is forced to pitch his appeal to a national electorate. However, any general appeal will undoubtedly receive a somewhat different reception in different parts of the country and in different states. For example, white men in New Hampshire may respond differently to a campaign message or to a candidate than white men in South Carolina. This section of the book examines the extent to which the two presidential campaigns in 2008 were able to successfully pitch the appeal of their national campaigns to groups in Florida. It compares the support that both Obama and McCain received from voting groups in Florida with the support from these same groups at the national level. The comparisons are shown in Table 6.2.

Since the overall margin of victory in Florida was smaller than that in the nation, it should come as no surprise that Barack Obama's margins within voting groups in this state would be more narrow than they were among these same groups at the national level and that McCain would show fewer and smaller differences between his performance in the nation and in Florida. Thirty four (34) groups were examined in the analysis. Obama did less well in Florida than in the nation in 19 of these groups. He did better in Florida than in the nation in 11 of the groups and in four there was no difference. McCain did less well in Florida than in the nation in 8 groups, better in 24 groups and equally well in 2 groups.

Even though Obama did less well in Florida than in the nation, the differences between his national and Florida support among the groups we examined were small. Nine groups gave him substantially poorer support (-5%) in Florida than in the nation and his poorest performance relative to the nation was among the income group $75,000–$99,900 (-12%) and first time voters (-10%). Only three groups gave him substantially greater support (5%+) in Florida than in the nation; those who did not complete high school, those who had a high school education only and the religious group that was something other than Protestant, Catholic or Jewish. In comparison to his national performance, he also did poorly among Florida's Hispanics population, -10%. Nevertheless, he won this group in Florida and as was seen in the preceding section, this performance was one of the critical elements in his victory in the state.

John McCain did better in Florida than in the nation as a whole, although the differences were not enough for him to carry the state. His best showing in Florida vis a vis the nation came among Hispanics where he polled 11 points higher, in the income group $75,000–$99,999 where he won 10% more votes

Table 6.2. Social Group Voting in Florida and the Nation (2008)

	Florida				Nation						
	McCain	Obama	Margin	Total	McCain	Obama	Margin	Total	Margin	Difference	%Difference
Gender											
Male	47	51	4	47	48	49	1	47	3	0.015253524	1.53%
Female	47	52	5	53	43	56	13	53	-8	-0.04040404	-4.04%
Race											
White	56	42	-14	71	55	43	-12	74	-2	-0.010204082	-1.02%
Black	4	96	92	13	4	95	91	13	1	0.00040404	0%
Hispanic/Latino	42	57	15	14	31	67	36	9	-21	-0.107915894	-10.79%
Asian	*	*		1	35	62	27	2			
Other	*	*		1	31	66	35	3			
Age											
18-29	37	61	24	15	32	66	34	18	-10	-0.051020408	-5.10%
30-44	49	49	0	25	46	52	6	29	-6	-0.030612245	-3.06%
45-64	47	52	5	37	49	50	1	37	4	0.02020202	2.02%
65+	53	45	-8	22	53	45	-8	16	0	0	0%
2007 Total Family Income											
Under $15,000	33	66	33	8	25	73	48	6	-15	-0.078231293	-7.82%
$15,000-$29,999	37	62	25	12	37	60	23	12	2	0.007705925	0.77%
$30,000-$49,999	39	59	20	19	43	55	12	19	8	0.040816327	4.08%
$50,000-$74,999	52	47	-5	23	49	48	-1	21	-4	-0.020097886	-2.01%
$75,000-$99,999	58	39	-19	14	48	51	3	15	-22	-0.113089659	-11.31%
$100,000-$149,999	58	40	-18	12	51	48	-3	14	-15	-0.07668522	-7.67%
$150,000-$199,999	54	45	-9	7	50	48	-2	6	-7	-0.035250464	-3.53%
$200,000 or more	48	51	3	5	46	52	6	6	-3	-0.01546073	-1.55%
Last Grade of School Completed											
Did not complete high school	29	70	41	3	35	63	28	4	13	0.064213564	6.42%
High school graduate	41	58	17	20	46	52	6	20	11	0.055246341	5.52%
Some college or associate degree	49	49	0	32	47	51	4	31	-4	-0.020408163	-2.04%
College graduate	53	45	-8	32	48	50	2	28	-10	-0.051020408	-5.10%
Postgraduate study	41	58	17	13	40	58	18	17	-1	-0.005978149	-0.60%
Party Identification											
Democrat	12	87	75	37	10	89	79	39	-4	0.101010101	10.10%
Republican	87	12	-75	34	90	9	-81	32	6	0.03030303	3.03%

(continued)

Table 8.1. *(Continued)*

Independent or something else	45	52	7	29	44	52	8	29	-1	-0.005584192	-0.56%
On Most Political Matters Consider Themselves:											
Liberal	8	91	83	19	10	89	79	22	4	0.02020202	2.02%
Moderate	41	57	16	47	39	60	21	44	-5	-0.024427953	-2.44%
Conservative	77	21	-56	35	78	20	-58	34	2	0.010204082	1.02%
First Time Voter											
Yes	40	59	19	12	30	69	39	11	-20	-0.10101010	-1.01%
No	48	50	2	88	48	50	2	89	0	0	0.00%
Religion, Combined Protestant and Other Christian											
Protestant/Other Christian	55	43	-12	52	54	45	-9	54	-3	-0.015769944	-1.58%
Catholic	49	50	1	28	45	54	9	27	-8	-0.04040404	-4.04%
Jewish	*	*		4	21	78	57	2			
Something else	18	80	62	6	22	73	51	6	11	0.047905478	4.79%
None	26	71	45	10	23	75	52	12	-7	-0.03334736	-3.34%

than in the nation and among first time voters where he also won 10% more voters in Florida than in the nation.

SUMMARY

Barack Obama won the presidential election in Florida because he was able to appeal to the great majority of the social groups that make up Florida's electorate. He achieved high levels of support from the state's minority population and from the baby boomer generation. In contrast, John McCain was unable to sustain the support of some of the critical elements of the Bush coalition, particularly Hispanics, conservatives and higher income voters.

Chapter Seven

Candidates and Issues in the 2008 Campaign

Voter attitudes toward the candidates, the public policy issues that concern the electorate and the political parties are widely thought to be the most important attitudes in shaping the vote. (Campbell, Converse, Miller and Stokes. 1961) This chapter examines the first two of these attitudes.

One of the most important elements in an election is the issues that concern the public. Each election presents a unique mixture of policy concerns and the strategies of the candidates regarding these issues are correspondingly unique. In some years economic concerns are most important in the minds of voters, in others it may be security issues or issues related to specific areas of public policy such as education or health care. As candidates offer remedies to the issues of the day, voters assess their promises, voting for the candidate whose policy solutions meet their own preferences. The issues in the 2008 election in Florida are examined in this section of the book.

THE CONCERNS OF THE ELECTORATE

In the 2006 Congressional elections, dissatisfaction with the war in Iraq helped Democrats gain control of Congress and suggested that foreign policy would be the dominant issue in the 2008 presidential election. However as the number of deaths in Iraq declined and the coverage of the issue by the news media decreased, polls began to indicate that Americans were more concerned about economic conditions than about the war and terrorism. By December of 2007, polls were showing that 73% of Americans felt that the economy was in bad shape and that this issue was their top concern, typically cited two or three times more often than the war in Iraq, health care or the environment. (www.america.gov/st/elections08-english/2008/august/20080815122222hmnietsua0.8663446.html) By the fall of 2008, experts were reporting that the economy was suffering its most serious downturn since the Great Depression, solidifying this issue as the most important in the election, both in the nation and in Florida.

In the aftermath of the election, exit polls confirmed these findings. According to those interviewed in Florida and in the nation as a whole, the condition of the economy was by far the most important issue facing the nation, six times more important than the next most important issues, the war in Iraq and terrorism. Other issues included health care and energy policy. The data, both for Florida and the nation, are shown in table 7.1.

Concern about these issues affected vote decisions. For example, voters in both Florida and the nation as a whole who thought that the condition of the nation's economy was poor were much more likely to vote for Barack Obama than for John McCain. And for those *very* worried about the economy (53% of the electorate), 59% said that they had voted for Obama. The data are shown in Table 7.2. The only other issue that benefitted Obama in Florida was concern about terrorism and 56% of those who saw this as the most important problem facing the nation voted for him as opposed to McCain.

On the other hand, voters who thought that the war in Iraq was the most important issue and those who strongly approved of the U.S. war in Iraq were more likely to vote for John McCain than for Barack Obama. Information about the relationship between a voter's positions on these issues and his or her vote decision is displayed in Table 7.3.

Voters in Florida and those in the nation as a whole responded to the foregoing issues somewhat differently even though their rankings of issue importance were almost identical. The issue of healthcare, in particular, brought out quite different voter responses in the state than it did in the country as a whole. In Florida those who thought it was the most important issue were overwhelmingly more likely to vote for John McCain than for

Table 7.1. Most Important Problems as Seen by the Electorate in Florida and the Nation. "Which one of these five issues is the most important facing the nation?"

	Florida			Nationwide		
	% Total	Obama	McCain	% Total	Obama	McCain
The War in Iraq	10	38	61	10	59	39
The Economy	62	60	39	63	53	44
Terrorism	10	56	42	9	13	86
Healthcare	8	8	92	9	73	26
Energy Policy	7	38	61	7	50	46

Table 7.2. Concern about the Economy. "How worried are you about the direction of the nation's economy in the next year?"

	% Total	Obama	McCain
Very worried	53	59	39
Somewhat worried	30	42	56
Not too worried	10	43	55

Barack Obama, while voters throughout the US who viewed this issue as most important were much more likely to vote for Obama. Ninety two percent (92%) of voters in Florida who saw healthcare as the most important issue said that they had voted for John McCain, while 73% of voters in the nation who ranked healthcare as the most important issue voted for Barack Obama.

A somewhat similar, and only slightly less dramatic, difference was apparent in the response of the two sets of voters to the issue of terrorism. In Florida, voters who saw this as the most important issue favored Obama, by 56% to 42%. In contrast, voters throughout the nation who saw this as the most important problem voted 86% to 13% for McCain. Finally, voters in the US who viewed energy policy as the most important issue facing the country were more likely to vote for Obama while those in Florida who saw this as the most important issue voted for John McCain.

The findings reported above suggest that the policy issues in the campaign were quite important to the outcome of the 2008 election and that the condition of the economy was critical to Obama's victory in Florida. With the exception of those who saw the economy as the most important issue and of the 10% of the electorate who saw terrorism as the most important issue, most voters in Florida saw John McCain as the candidate closest to them and therefore cast their ballot for him. These findings seem to verify what many

Table 7.3. Concern about the War in Iraq. "How do you feel about the US war in Iraq?"

	% Total	Obama	McCain
Strongly approve	19	3	97
Somewhat approve	23	19	80
Somewhat disapprove	17	58	38
Strongly disapprove	40	89	9

analysts suggested after the votes were cast; that whatever chance John McCain had of becoming president disappeared in the aftermath of the dramatic September, 15, 2008 collapse of Lehman Brothers and McCain's subsequent statement at a rally in Florida that the "fundamentals of our economy are strong." Within days of this remark, Obama was on the campaign trail mocking McCain's comment and suggesting that he, like President Bush, was deeply out of touch on the nation's economy.

Presidential Performance, Candidate Qualities and Electoral Behavior

When making electoral decisions, voters look not only at the positions that candidates take on the important issues of the day but also at the performance of the incumbent and at particular attributes of the candidates. In the 2008 presidential election, there is a strong case to be made that the incumbent, George Bush, and his administration "established directly and indirectly the agenda for the presidential campaign. " (Crotty. 2008) As shown above, the issues generated by the Bush presidency—the conduct of the wars in Iraq and on terrorism and an economy in deep trouble—dominated the discussion in the campaign and the president's handling of these issues and his job as president became the fulcrum of the Obama message, "Change."

Presidential Job Performance

The perception by Floridians of how well George Bush performed his job as president was closer to how the nation as a whole perceived him than it was to how other Southern states viewed this performance. The average approval rating in nine other Southern states was 37% In Florida the rating was 28% and in the nation as a whole it was 27%. (Calculated from data in Todd and Sheldon. 2009) Seventy percent (70%) of Floridians and 71% of the nation as a whole disapproved of the performance. In Florida 52% *strongly* disapproved of Bush's performance, higher even than the number in the nation as a whole where the "strongly disapprove" level was 51%. The last time an incumbent president had an approval rating this low in an election year was 1952 when Harry Truman found support among only 22% of the electorate.

These views about the president dominated voter decision making in Florida and led McCain to protest "I'm not President Bush." Nevertheless, "Floridians voted almost as if he was," and in the end retrospective evaluation of Bush's performance outweighed the importance of any issue of concern to the Florida public. (Martinez. 2009) Large majorities of those who disapproved of the president's job performance supported Barack Obama. The numbers were 67% in the U.S. and 69% in Florida. Given the public's view of the president's job performance, it is understandable that the McCain campaign spent much of the campaign trying to disassociate himself from Bush. In the end, 47% of the Florida electorate and 48% of the national electorate thought McCain would continue in the direction set by President Bush and of those who felt this way, nine out of ten voted for Obama.

CANDIDATE QUALITIES

In addition to the performance of the incumbent president, a number of characteristics of the two presidential candidates themselves may also have affected vote choice in the 2008 election. These were the race of the individuals involved, their relative levels of experience, and how they conducted their campaigns.

Race

As the first African-American candidate for president who had a serious chance of winning, Barack Obama was the target of intense public interest and there was much public satisfaction that race relations in the United States had finally evolved to the point where a black person had a realistic chance of becoming president. Nevertheless, racial hatred still exists, both in Florida and in the United States, and Mr. Obama received 500 death threats during his presidential campaign. In response to such threats, the secret service placed him under its protection on May 3, 2007, the earliest ever for a presidential candidate. In light of the history of racism in the U.S., there was, of course, concern that Obama's race would be a factor in whether or not people would cast their vote for him.

On the surface, at least, this concern appears to have been misplaced, both in Florida and in the nation. Exit polls show that 83% of the Florida electorate and 90% of that in the United States as a whole said that race was not an important factor in deciding their vote. Furthermore, the differences in the vote choices between those who said that race was an important factor and those who said it was not, were insignificant. Among those in the national electorate for whom race was an important factor, Obama got 53% of the vote and among those for whom race was not a factor Obama received 52% of the vote. For Floridians, the differences were almost the same. As shown in Table 7.4, for those who thought race was an important factor, 54% voted for Obama and for those who said race was not an important factor, 51% voted for Obama.

Table 7.4. Concern about the Race of the Candidates in Florida and the Nation. "In deciding your vote, was the race of the candidates an important factor for you?"

	Florida			Nationwide		
	% Total	Obama	McCain	% Total	Obama	McCain
Important factor	15	54	45	9	53	46
Not an important factor	83	51	48	90	52	46

Experience vs. Change

The mantra of the Obama campaign was change, and change meant disassociation with all things George Bush and the Republican Party. Obama campaigned relentlessly on this message and was successful in turning it into the candidate quality that was the most important to voters when making their electoral decision. Thirty four percent (34%) of both the Florida and the national electorate said that the ability to bring about change was the most important quality to them, with only 23% saying experience was most important. Ninety two percent of those who cited the need for change as the most important quality for a presidential candidate cast their vote for Barack Obama.

Despite McCain campaign attempts to portray Obama as lacking the experience to be president, 81% of the Florida electorate and 85% of the national electorate said that both candidates had the "experience to serve effectively as president."

Negative Advertising

While Americans report in poll after poll that they dislike attack ads, there is substantial evidence these ads often can be effective and they have become a regular part of political campaigns throughout the nation. The analysis in Chapter III of this book shows that both John McCain and Barack Obama employed the techniques, with McCain relying on them exclusively. The questions addressed here are whether or not the candidates were perceived as using negative ads and whether or not their use had an effect on the outcome of the election. Table 7.5 shows data related to these questions.

Most voters, both in Florida and in the nation, thought that both candidates employed negative ads, but more voters felt that John McCain was the greater user. Sixty four percent (64%) felt that McCain had conducted unfair attacks, and 48% thought Obama had done so. The data also suggest that use of the ads had a negative effect on vote choice; for voters who thought that only Barack Obama attacked John McCain unfairly, 89% voted for McCain and

Table 7.5. Concern about Negative Ads. "Did either of these candidates for president attack the other unfairly?"

	% Total	Obama	McCain
Only Barack Obama	9	10	89
Only John McCain	25	99	1
Both of them	39	39	59
Neither of them	23	38	61

the reverse was true for voters who thought that only John McCain attacked Obama unfairly. In this case 90% voted for Obama.

McCain suffered the most damage from the perception that he used negative ads. Of the voters who thought that neither candidate attacked the other unfairly, McCain received a majority of the vote, both in Florida and in the nation. This raises the possibility that had he avoided an exclusive reliance on negative campaigning, he might have gained votes.

Part III

THE CONGRESSIONAL ELECTIONS

Chapter Eight

The Outcome of the 2008 Congressional Races

INTRODUCTION

While the presidential election was the dominant feature of the 2008 electoral cycle, Floridians also cast ballots in twenty-five elections for U.S. Congress and this section examines the patterns and trends in these elections.

Despite their strong statewide position, Democrats are not in the majority in every Congressional and state legislative district and in the run up to the 2008 elections Republicans controlled 16 of the 25 Congressional seats, 26 of the 40 State Senate seats and 77 of the 120 State House seats. In the 2008 Congressional and state legislative elections, the Republicans continued this dominance, losing one seat in Congress and one seat in the State House of Representatives. Part of the analysis provided here is an exploration of why the presidential results were not manifested at the Congressional and state legislative levels and of the implications of this result.

Unlike many smaller states whose populations change very little over time, Florida has seen huge population shifts over the past 50 years and the state's Congressional delegation has grown accordingly when districts were reapportioned every 10 years. In 1950, the state had 8 members of Congress. By 2002, this number had risen to 25 and had increased every decade during that time period. During this same time period, the once complete domination of the Democratic Party declined. In 1950, Florida was a one party Democratic state with all 8 members of the Congressional delegation elected from that party. The size of the Democratic majority declined in every decade after that time and in 1990, the Republicans finally wrested control of the delegation from the Democrats. It has remained in the majority since that time. Table 8.1 shows the distribution of seats over the time period 1980 to 2008.

Table 8.1. Distribution of Congressional Seats in Florida by Party (1952–2006)

		Republicans		*Democrats*	
Year	Districts	Number	Percent	Number	Percent
1952	8	0	0.0	8	100.0
1954	8	1	12.5	7	87.5
1956	8	1	12.5	7	87.5
1958	8	1	12.5	7	87.5
1960	8	1	12.5	7	87.5
			10.0		**90.0**
1962	12	2	16.7	10	83.3
1964	12	2	16.7	10	83.3
1966	12	3	25.0	9	75.0
1968	12	3	25.0	9	75.0
1970	12	3	25.0	9	75.0
			21.7		**78.3**
1972	15	4	26.7	11	73.3
1974	15	5	33.3	10	66.7
1976	15	5	33.3	10	66.7
1978	15	3	20.0	12	80.0
1980	15	4	26.7	11	73.3
			28.0		**72.0**
1982	19	6	31.6	13	68.4
1984	19	7	36.8	12	63.2
1986	19	7	36.8	12	63.2
1988	19	9	47.4	10	52.6
1990	19	10	52.6	9	47.4
			41.1		**58.9**
1992	23	13	56.5	10	43.5
1994	23	15	65.2	8	34.8

Table 8.1. *(Continued)*

1996	23	15	65.2	8	34.8
1998	23	15	65.2	8	34.8
2000	23	15	65.2	8	34.8
			63.5		**36.5**
2002	25	18	72.0	7	28.0
2004	25	18	72.0	7	28.0
2006	25	15	60.0	10	40.0
			68.0		**32.0**

When the Republicans gained majority status in the 1990 elections, the state had 19 congressional representatives and the Republicans won victories in 10 of these seats (52.6%). After an increase in delegation size to 23 and the accompanying reapportionment in 1992, the Republicans continued their dominance and won 13 of these seats (56.5%). They increased their numbers to 15 in 1994 (65.2%). This distribution continued throughout the decade. In 2002, the delegation increased to 25, the districts were reapportioned and the Republicans won 18 seats or 72.0%. It held this majority until 2006 when all Democratic incumbents held their seats and Democratic challengers defeated two Republican incumbents, changing the composition to 16 Republicans to 9 Democrats and the percentages to 64% Republican to 36% Democrat.

In spite of a majority of registered Democrats in the state as a whole, when the 2008 electoral cycle opened in Florida, a majority of the state's congressional districts leaned toward the Republican Party. Voter registration figures put the Republicans in a favorable position; 17 of the 25 districts had a majority of registered Republicans. Furthermore, 17 of the 25 congressional districts had an R+ value on the Cook Partisan Voting Index. This index is a measurement of competitiveness, of how strongly a congressional district leans toward one party compared to its leaning in the nation as a whole. Districts with + values are those in which presidential candidates perform better in the district than at the national level. For example, a PVI score of R+2 shows that recent Republican presidential candidates received 2 percentage points more votes in the relevant district than he did in the nation as a whole. Thus a district with an R+15 is a district that voted 15 percentage points (as an average of its previous two presidential votes) higher for the Republican candidate than the percentage of the national vote in the most recent presidential election. In 2008, the national range on the index was D+41 in New

York's 15th and 16th districts to R+29 in Alabama's 6th and Texas' 13th. As the 2008 election began in Florida the range was D+35 in District 17 to R+19 in District 1.

It is, of course possible for a candidate of a party to win a seat in which the other party has a partisan advantage, but it is unusual for this to take place when the majority party has a + value of 6 or higher on the PVI. Plus values lower than 6 are thought to indicate relative vulnerability for the incumbent.

DISTRICT BY DISTRICT ANALYSIS

As the 2008 electoral cycle opened, there was reason to believe that a substantial change in the partisan complexion of the Florida delegation might be forthcoming. The two seats won in 2006 by Democrats Tim Mahoney in the 16th district (R+5) and by Ron Klein in the 22nd (D+1) appeared sustainable for the Democrats. A third candidate who had lost in 2006 by 369 votes was to make another run at the 13th district (R+6), and the Democrats were mounting strong candidates in three other districts with potential for them, the 8th (R+2) the 15th (R+6) and the 24th (R+4). Further, changes in the Hispanic population—increases in non-Cubans—in the three South Florida Hispanic districts (18, 21 and 25) put these "in play." No other incumbents appeared vulnerable and victory in all the above races would have given the Democrats a majority in the congressional delegation. In what follows, the races in each district are examined.

District 1

Florida's First Congressional district covers the western part of Florida's Panhandle. It stretches from Pensacola to the Alabama border and portions are in the Central Time Zone, rather than the Eastern Zone along with the rest of Florida. It includes large active duty Air Force and Navy populations as well as substantial numbers of retired military.

District 1 is very conservative and has not voted for a Democratic presidential candidate since 1960. In 1964, Barry Goldwater carried the district by such a large margin that it almost tipped the election in Florida into the hands of the Republicans. Nevertheless, it continued to elect conservative congressional Democrats until the 1994 Republican Revolution, when Joe Scarborough became the first Republican ever elected to the seat. Since then the District has become the state's most reliably Republican district, electing Republicans to all levels of state and local government. It is not a seat that the Democrats aspire to and the current Congressman, Jeff Miller, who was first elected in 2002, has faced only token opposition from the Democrats since. In 2008, his margin of victory was 70.2% to 29.8%.

District 2

This district includes all or parts of 14 counties, including most of Leon which is the home of Tallahassee, the state capital. It is the classic old South, "cotton fields, soft pine stands, catfish farms, large families, small towns with large churches." (Barone. 2004, 393) Although voter registration favors the Democrats, many of these voters have long since left the Party philosophically and regularly vote for Republican presidential candidates. In 2004 and 2008, only three of the counties, Leon, home of Florida State University, Florida A&M University and Tallahassee Community College, Gadsen, the state's only black-majority county, and Jefferson, a small island of moderation in a sea of conservatism, voted for the Democratic presidential candidates.

The incumbent Congressman was Democrat Alan Boyd, a farmer from Jefferson County, who was first elected to an open seat in 1996, when the incumbent Democrat resigned. Subsequently, Congressman Boyd has developed one of the most centrist voting records in the House of Representatives and has become a leader in the conservative Blue Dog caucus. His voting record and his attention to his constituency have made him a difficult target for the Republicans who think they can win this seat (it was R+6 after the 2008 election) if he were to step aside. In 2002, the Republican controlled state legislature made the district a bit more Republican by adding Republican counties in the western part of the district and by dividing Boyd's own home town (population 3,000+/-) into two districts. Nevertheless, Boyd won, and continues to win, usually by a margin of two to one. While he has run unopposed only once in his career, the Republicans have essentially given up on beating him and did not provide serious backing to their candidate in 2008. Boyd won by 61.9% to 38.1%.

District 3

The 3rd Congressional district in Florida was created in 1992 to be North Florida's black majority seat. It includes the center of Jacksonville, and meanders South through Gainesville, includes the farming communities of Zellwood and Eatonville, the home of author Zora Neale Hurston, and ends up in downtown Orlando. Since 1992, it has seen its boundaries changed three times in order to shift as many Democrats as possible away from the surrounding Republican counties and make these Republican counties safer for that Party. This strategy has been successful in making it a "safe" Democratic seat. In 2008, it had 240,000 registered Democrats and 72,000 Republicans and was 49.3% black and 8% Hispanic. It had a D+16 on Cooks PVI. Nevertheless, the person who has held the seat since its inception, Corrine Brown, has been dogged by controversy throughout her tenure and has thus invited challenges from both Republicans and Democrats.

Brown, a former state legislator, was first elected in 1992 and a few weeks later, the Federal Elections Commission began investigating her for irregularities in her campaign. Other allegations were investigated in 1996 and again in 2000. These allegations spurred the Republicans to nominate and support qualified black candidates and to run against Brown's alleged ethical shortcomings. Over the time period 1994 to 2002, in a heavily Democratic district, the Republicans averaged 42% of the vote against her, but were not able to get over the line to victory. Finally, the Duval County Republican Chairman tired of his lack of success and said "I would rather not give Corrine Brown an excuse to go through another massive voter turnout exercise in which she is very talented" (*Jacksonville Free Press*. 2002) and Brown ran unopposed in 2004, 2006 & 2008.

District 4

In 1992, when the state legislature carved out downtown Jacksonville to help create the black majority 3rd district, it left the remainder of Duval county to the Republicans. A large portion of the county was combined with a series of small, rural counties that run along the Georgia border for over a hundred miles into Leon County and into Monticello, the 3,000 person home town of 2nd district Congressman Alan Boyd, to form District 4. About 70% of the population of the district is in Jacksonville and Nashua County, just to the North. Nashua and the remaining counties in the district are typical southern, conservative constituencies which, when combined with a heavy military presence and a number of large corporations in Jacksonville, make the district solidly Republican. In 2008, it had a R+16 PVI.

The incumbent congressman in the district is Ander Crenshaw, the son-in-law of the state's first Republican governor, and a former State legislator. Over the years Mr. Crenshaw ran unsuccessfully for three statewide offices, Florida Secretary of State, the U.S. Senate and Governor. He first ran for his House seat in 2000 when the Republican incumbent retired. He won the primary in that year by 70% to 30% and the general election by 67% to 31%. A reliable conservative, he has run mostly unopposed since his first election and had minimal opposition in 2008. He won by 65.3% to 34.7%.

District 5

This district lies on the Gulf Coast and includes Levy, Citrus, Hernando, Sumter, Pasco and parts of Marion and Lake counties. The district is populated to a large extent by retirees and in 2006 had 251,000 Social Security recipients, more than any other congressional district in the nation. The massive retirement community known as the "Villages" is the focal point for these retirees.

District 5 was drawn in 2002 to give Republicans an advantage over the Democratic incumbent Karen Thurman. The current incumbent, Ginny Brown-Waite had been elected to the State Senate in 1992 and had been asked to run for the congressional seat in 1996, but did not think it winnable. Subsequently, she used her position as a member of the Senate congressional re-districting committee to influence the parameters of the district and took on the race in 2002.

The 2002 campaign was one of the most competitive in the nation and brought both national political parties into the fray. Thurman outspent Brown-Waite by a two to one margin, but Brown-Waite was able to get President Bush to campaign on her behalf and the strong showing by Governor Jeb Bush in his re-election campaign also helped her. In the end, the decisions made by Brown-Waite's reapportionment committee proved decisive. Thurman carried the sections of the district she had formerly represented, which made up 49% of the vote, but Brown-Waite won the new parts of the district by 53% to 41% and won the election by 47.9% to 46.2%.

Although her narrow victory made her somewhat shaky, the Democrats could not get a strong candidate to run against her in 2004 (Thurman refused) and she won by 65.9% to 34.1%. Subsequently she has won handily and in 2008 cruised home by 61.2% to 38.8%. Despite these margins, the district remains competitive with a R+5 PVI and Democrats are always on the look for good candidates to throw into the battle.

District 6

This district is in central Florida and stretches from Duval County in the North to Marion and Sumter counties in the South, around Ocala. While it does include parts of Alachua County, home to the University of Florida and one of the most reliably Democratic counties in the state, it is an R+8 district and, especially around Ocala, is heavily Republican.

In 2008, the incumbent in this district was Republican Cliff Stearns. Stearns was first elected in 1988 and has become an active and conservative legislator. When first elected he promised to serve only 6 terms. While he broke that promise, he has not suffered and has run unopposed and against minimal competition. In 2008, he won by 60.9% to 39.1%.

District 7

This district runs for about 100 miles along Florida's Atlantic coastline and includes some of the oldest communities in Florida and in the nation. It begins just south of Jacksonville at Ponte Vedra Beach and continues south to Daytona Beach. It includes St Augustine, the nation's oldest permanent European settlement and Ormond Beach, where John D. Rockefeller "wintered." It also includes some newly developed areas more typical of "modern" Florida; the Palm Coast beach development in Flagler County and Deltona, built on a drained swamp in Volusia County. About two thirds of the vote resides in the counties around Orlando and Daytona Beach.

District 7 is potentially very competitive. It has a slight Republican edge in voter registration (214,273 to 191, 879) and a R+4 PVI, but has been represented since 1992 by Republican John Mica, who has had very little opposition over that time period. Mica, whose brother was once a Democratic Congressman from south Florida, has averaged 64% of the vote in the races in which he has been opposed. In 2008, he won 62% of the vote.

District 8

Congressional District 8 is the Disney district. It covers a narrow stretch of Central Florida that starts in Marion County runs through Lake County and ends in Orlando and Orange County with the Walt Disney World complex, the Disney owned town of Celebration, and Sea World and Universal Studios. In the 1980's the district was heavily Republican, but began to shift toward the Democrats in the 1990's as non-Cuban Hispanics and other working class people began to assimilate in Orange County, many of them to work at Disney. Over the time period 1980 to 2000, the district was held by Bill McCullom, a conservative Republican who had been one of the House Managers, or prosecutors, at Bill Clinton's impeachment trial.

When McCullom resigned in 2000 to run for the U.S. Senate, both political parties saw potential in the seat. Voter registration gave the Republicans a slight edge (about 15,000) votes, but the change that had taken place in the District demography gave the Democrats hope. Plus the party had a strong candidate in former Orange County Commission Chairman Linda Chapin.

The Republicans ran attorney Ric Keller who had gotten through a tough Republican primary with the help of a $400,000 contribution from Grover Norquist and the highly conservative Club for Growth. In the general election, Keller played up his anti-tax views and promised that if elected he would serve no more than four terms. He pulled out a 50.8% to 49.2% victory that left the Democrats deeply disappointed and determined to take a seat that they now thought, on the basis of the change in the district's demographics, was theirs. Nevertheless, Keller held the seat over the next eight years.

As the campaign opened in 2008, the Democrats had opened a slight advantage in voter registration (176,483 to 167,240), and the district carried a competitive R+3 PVI rating. Thus, when Keller reneged on his promise not to serve more than four terms and announced for re-election the Democrats saw a chance to pick up a Congressional seat. After a spirited primary the party selected Alan Grayson a Harvard educated attorney who had made a name for himself by repeatedly suing Iraqi contractors on behalf of whistle-blowers. His campaign against Keller featured a number of highly publicized ads focusing on military contractor fraud and he raised $3.2 million dollars for his campaign, in contrast to the $1.6 million garnered by Keller. He won the election by 52% to 48% of the vote. Although Keller won 3 out of the 4 counties in the district, Grayson won by 10% in Orange County, Orlando, by far the largest county in the district. This victory represented the gain of a Congressional seat that that the Florida Democrats thought they could count on holding for some time to come.

District 9

This district was created in 1982 and was drawn to be a Democratic seat. It begins on the Gulf Coast in Pasco County and travels south into part of Pinellas County and into central Florida and Hillsboro County, one of the counties that Obama flipped in 2008. It includes the towns of Jasmine Estates, New Port Richey, Tarpon Springs and Clearwater, among others.

A conservative area, the 9th district was represented from its inception through 2004 by Michael Bilirakis, a Democrat turned Republican who seldom faced serious opposition. In 2006, the senior Bilirakis was succeeded by his son, Gus Michael Bilirakis, who won re-election in 2008 by a vote of 62.2% to 37.8%.

District 10

Florida Congressional District 10 is the only district in the state that is located entirely in one county, in this case Pinellas, a county that shifted from the Republicans to the Democrats in 2008. The dominant political entity is the City of St Petersburg. The district was the first to elect a Republican, William Cramer, to Congress in 1952, but had trended Democratic over the years. In 1970, when the seat was vacated by Cramer his place was taken by Bill Young, who has held the seat since that time. Young is a moderate conservative who has held important positions of leadership in the U.S. House of Representatives, including Chair of the Appropriations Committee.

Over the years, the Republicans in the state legislature have tried to make the seat more Republican, but by 2008, they had a voter registration margin of only 170,000 to 164,000 over the Democrats and a PVI of R+3. Nevertheless, political developments in the district have had little effect on Bill Young and in the 10 years leading up to 2008, he was unopposed twice and when challenged won by an average of 70% of the vote. In 2008 he was re-elected by a margin of 60.7% to 39.3%. Until Young retires, the Democrats have little chance in this district.

District 11

This district is centered in Tampa, but also includes close-in suburbs, neighborhoods on the east shore of Tampa Bay and two areas on the west side of Tampa Bay. This is a heavily Democratic district, with a voter registration margin of more than two to one. It is ranked as D+11 on the PVI.

The current incumbent is Kathy Castor, daughter of Betty Castor, for 35 years a major figure in Florida Democratic politics, who lost the U.S. Senate seat in 2004 very narrowly to Republican Mel Martinez. Kathy Castor won the District 11 seat in 2006 when Jim Davis, who had held the position since 1996, resigned to run for Governor. She won re-election in 2008 with 71% of the vote.

District 12

Congressional district 12 is located in North central Florida and includes Polk County and parts of Osceola and Hillsborough counties. It is the classic southern agricultural county, growing strawberries, citrus and tomatoes and raising cattle.

District 12 has a Democratic majority, but was last represented by a member of that party in 1978. Like many rural districts in the South, its conservative constituencies have voted for Republicans who have championed their strong defense, "family values" positions.

Since 2000 the 12th district had been represented by Adam Putnam, a fifth-generation Floridian and farmer who has been a consistent supporter of the George Bush administration approach to government and of the complete Bush agenda. Indeed, he was with President Bush in Sarasota, Florida on the morning of September 11, 2001 when the World Trade Towers were attacked.

Putnam has rarely had serious opposition in contests for re-election and won in 2008 by 15 percentage points, his closest race since his initial victory in 2000.

District 13

This district covers all of Sarasota County which includes the Cities of Sarasota and of Venice and the rural areas of Hardee, DeSoto and Manatee counties. It is very wealthy and very Republican.

Since 1984, when Andy Ireland, who had been elected as a Democrat switched to the Republican Party, it has been represented by members of the GOP. Daniel Miller took Ireland's place in 1992 and served for the following 10 years. His resignation in 2002 sparked a series of political battles that lasted over a period of four years.

The first person to declare their candidacy for the vacancy in 2002 was the sitting Secretary of State of Florida, Katherine Harris. Harris, who was the scion of an extremely wealthy old Florida family, had been the co-chair of the Bush/Cheney election campaign in 2000 and had come under massive criticism for her role in the recount of the Florida vote in that election. She created immediate controversy in the Congressional race when she violated Florida law by failing to resign from Secretary of State before filing for the 13th District seat. Nevertheless, she went on to win the Republican primary handily.

Assuming that Harris's notoriety made her vulnerable, the Democrats mounted a serious campaign and selected as their candidate Jan Schneider, a Washington lobbyist who had been a law school classmate of Bill and Hillary Clinton. Harris won by 55% to 45%, but in light of her name recognition, her financial resources and the nature of the district, the results were disappointing for the Republicans. They also gave heart to Schneider who challenged Harris again in 2004, only to lose by the same margin as in 2002.

After serving two terms in the House, Harris resigned in 2004 to run for the U.S. Senate against the Democratic incumbent Bill Nelson and created an open seat in the 13th District. In light of their experience against Harris, the Democrats held out hope of picking up this seat and looked for a strong candidate. Jan Schneider was again interested in the seat, but the Democrats pushed Christine Jennings, a retired Sarasota bank executive, who won the primary. Sensing a problem, the Republicans put up Vern Buchanan, a wealthy automobile dealer who contributed more than $5 million of his own money to the campaign and outspent Jennings by over $8 million to $3 million. In addition the Republicans brought in their heaviest guns in support. In the last month of the campaign, with polls showing Jennings ahead, Vice President Dick Cheney, President George Bush, Governor Jeb Bush, U.S. Senator Mel Martinez and Massachusetts Governor Mitt Romney all came to the 13th district to support Buchanan.

The outcome of the race was reminiscent of the 2000 presidential race in Florida when problems with voting technology clouded the results. A faulty machine in one part of the district failed to cast 18,000 voters for either of the congressional candidates and more votes were given to a hospital board race than to the Congressional candidates. About 13% of the electorate in Sarasota County failed to vote in this election, creating a serious undervote in a very close election which Buchanan won by 369 votes. Subsequent research into the causes of the voting machine failure attributed it to faulty ballot screen layout and suggested that had the 18,000 votes that had not registered because of this error been counted, Schneider would have won by 639 votes. (Ash and Lampeti. 2008)

This background provided the context for the 2008 race. While Ms Jennings was unsuccessful in her challenge of the 2006 outcome, she was retired, wealthy and harbored the impression that she had won that race. Thus, she decided to run again in 2008 and the Democrats were optimistic that they could add this seat to their numbers.

They were too optimistic and the district is too Republican (Republican registered voters outnumber Democrats by 219,776 to 167,843). Despite mounting a more aggressively negative campaign and raising $1 million more in campaign funds than she had in 2006, the sizeable Republican advantage in the district could not be overcome. Buchanan rallied the Republicans to his cause and defeated Ms Jennings by 63% to 37%.

District 14

This district is another heavily Republican district (R+10) that is dominated by affluent retirees in the Gulf Coast towns of Naples, Bradenton and Cape Coral who came from the Midwest and Northwest to take advantage of Florida's favorable tax structure.

Between 1988 and 2004, the district had been represented by Porter Goss, Chairman of the House Intelligence Committee and one of the most conservative members of the House of Representatives. In July, 2004, Goss resigned the seat to accept an appointment to become Director of the CIA and triggered a substantial intraparty battle among Republicans.

One of the first candidates to file was Connie Mack IV, son of the man who had represented the district for three terms in the 1980s and who had gone on to be elected to the U.S. Senate.

Connie, IV had been born in the district but had subsequently moved across the state and had been elected to a State House seat in Broward and Palm Beach counties. On announcement of the vacancy in the 14th, Mack resigned this House seat, moved to the district in Lee County and announced his candidacy for Congress. Three other Republicans also filed; a Lee County Commissioner, a state Representative and a Naples physician. All three attacked Mack as a carpetbagger and derided his campaign tactics which included sending Hooters girls to charity events. Nevertheless, his name and his ability to raise money (he outpaced his nearest rival by two to one) led him to a narrow 4% victory. He won the general election by 68% to 32%.

The Republicans apparently settled their intraparty dispute in 2006 and Mack faced no Republican primary opposition in 2008. The Democrats seem also to have conceded this seat and Mack went on to win re-election in the general election, with 59.4% to 24.8% for his Democratic opponent and the remainder two people running as No Party Affiliation, including one former Republican.

District 15

Congressional district 15 in Florida is an R+4 PVI district that runs from Vero Beach to Merritt Island along the Atlantic coast. The Republicans enjoy a 199,669 to 183,100 registered voter advantage. In 2008 it had been in the hands of Republican Dave Weldon for seven terms. Early in that year, Weldon, who had won 56.3% of the vote in 2006, announced that he would retire at the end of the term. In light of the relative competitiveness of the district, this resignation sparked primary fights in both parties. Ultimately the Republicans selected State Senator Bill Posey and the Democrats chose Steve Blythe, an MD who emphasized health care issues. Two other candidates ran as Independents.

During the campaign, both major candidates said that they would vote for the other if they couldn't vote for themselves. Nevertheless, Blythe took a variety of very liberal positions in what was a very conservative district. He supported nationalized health care and suggested that Nancy Pelosi, the Satan of the conservatives in America, was too soft on some issues. Topping Posey's campaign platform was fiscal legislation and strong stands on national security. In addition he supported completion of the border fence between Mexico and the U.S., as well as a bill to immediately deport all criminal aliens. Furthermore, he raised nearly 9 times the amount of money as did Blythe. He won the election by 53.1% to 42%.

District 16

This is an oddly shaped district that covers all or parts of eight counties and stretches across the central part of the state from the Atlantic to the Gulf Coast. While the district has been in the hands of the Republicans for more than 20 years, in 2006, the Republicans had a voter registration advantage of only 52% to 48% and the district carried a competitive R+2 PVI.

In 2006, the district became the site of one of the most visible political events in the nation when the incumbent Congressman, Mark Foley, was caught in the glare of a scandal with sexual overtones that involved male teen aged Pages in the U.S. House of Representatives. In the aftermath, and late in September during his campaign for re-election, Foley resigned and the Republicans replaced him with State Representative Joe Negron. Unfortunately for Negron, Florida law prohibited Foley's name from being removed from the ballot and supporters of Negron had to vote for Foley.

Compounding the Republican's problems, the Democrats had already recruited a strong candidate in Tim Mahoney, a wealthy businessman who had once been a Republican. Mahoney raised about two times the money as did Negron, slipped into the office by a margin of 49.5% to 47.7% and became the first Democrat to represent the district since its creation in 1973 (it changed numbers in both 1983 and 1993).

The scandal associated with this loss by Foley was thought by some to have contributed to the Republican Party's loss of control over Congress in the 2006 election and, when combined with the defeat of Republican Clay Shaw in the states' 22nd district, cut the Republican majority in Florida to 16 to 9. This gain was to be short lived.

As the 2008 campaign began, the Republicans were determined to re-gain the seat and recruited Tom Rooney, a local attorney whose family owns the Pittsburgh Steelers. Vice President Dick Cheney came into the state to campaign on behalf of Rooney and by early August, Rooney had raised more than $800,000.

Nevertheless, Mahoney had made a major effort to sell himself as a moderate and had secured an endorsement from the NRA. He led in the polls and was raising substantial money on his own. Then, on October 13, *ABC News* reported that Mahoney had agreed to pay a former mistress $121,000 in order to prevent her from suing him for sexual harassment. Relatively soon in the aftermath of this revelation, the polls quickly changed in favor of Rooney and he was elected by a margin of 60.1% to 39.9%, regaining the seat the Republicans had lost in 2006 and probably closing off any possibilities in the district for Democrats in the foreseeable future (assuming no more scandals).

District 17

This district is located in metropolitan Miami. It stretches from the Miami Arena in downtown Miami north through Allapattah and Liberty City to Opa-Locka. It is 55% African-American and has the fewest number of registered Republicans, 37,502 in 2008, of any district in the State. In 2006, it had a D+35 PVI.

Beginning with the creation of the district in its present form it has been represented by the Meek family, mother and son. Carrie Meek was first elected in 1992 and served without serious opposition until 2002. In July of that year, just two weeks before the filing deadline, she announced she would not run again and that she would campaign instead for her son, Kendrick. Kendrick Meek had served in the Florida House of Representatives and in the State Senate and was a visable political figure in his own right. He was elected without opposition in 2002 and has been re-elected in that fashion since.

District 18

This district is also wholly within Miami, but in a decidedly different section of the city than District 17. Whereas District 17 is a majority African-American, the 18th is about 6% black, but about 63% Hispanic. Whereas District 17 includes some of the city's poorest residents, District 18 covers some of the area's wealthiest communities, including Coral Gables, Cocoplum and Key Biscayne.

The District has been represented since 1989 by Ileana Ros-Lehtinen, a Republican who was the first Hispanic woman ever elected to the U.S. Congress. Ros-Lehtinen had been a member of the Florida State House of Representatives and of the Florida State Senate and ran for Congress upon the death of the long-time incumbent, Claude Pepper, a Florida political icon.

Her first election remains one of the classic political battles in Florida history. It pitted Ros-Lehtinen against Democrat Gerald Richman, a prominent Jewish lawyer who had been the president of the American Bar Association. The election took place just as the Hispanic community, and in particular the Cubans, was coming to political ascendancy and when the Republicans took anti-Castro positions that were to solidify that group's support for the next 20 years.

After a divisive race that included charges of racial bigotry against both campaigns, Ros-Lehtinen won with 53% of the vote. Turnout in Hispanic precincts was especially high (70% in Little Havana) and Hispanic voters split 94% to 6% percent for Ros-Lehtinen. Richman carried all other blocs of voters, Jewish, Anglos, and Blacks, but they constituted only 47% of the electorate. (See Moreno and Rae)

Ros-Lehtinen has run against weak opposition since her first election, but the Democrats have never completely given up on this seat and as the Cuban community ages and other Hispanic groups moved to Florida and identified with the Democrats, this district became more competitive. Ros-Lehtinen won by her smallest margin ever in 2008, 59.9% to 42.1% and in 2008 the Cook Political Report rated the district as R+3, very competitive.

District 19

The 19th District is another that was drawn to pack heavy Democratic totals in one part of the state—here in heavily Jewish communities that ran north from Ft Lauderdale through West Palm Beach, Margate, Mission Bay and Boca Raton—in order to free up Republicans to be sprinkled around other districts. In 2008, the district had 231,439 registered Democrats and 114,504 Republicans and a D+15 PVI.

While the district supported George Bush in both 2000 and 2004, the incumbent Democrat, Robert Wexler has won handily since his first election in 1990. In that first contest he garnered 66% of the vote and has averaged 70% since then, when opposed. In 2008, he won 66.2%.

District 20

District 20 covers parts of two counties in South Florida: Broward and Miami-Dade. Like the 19th district, it is heavily Jewish and the gay/lesbian community in Wilton Manors is said to be the third largest as a percentage of total community population in the nation. It was obviously drawn as a Democratic district; it has 204,200 registered Democrats and 104,102 Republicans and in 2008 had a D+13 PVI. In 2008 it was represented by Debbie Wasserman-Schultz.

Ms. Wasserman-Schultz was first elected to Congress in 2004 after serving 12 years in the Florida legislature, both in the House and the Senate. In 1992 at age 26 she was the youngest woman ever elected to the Florida House. She ran unopposed in the Democratic primary in her initial Congressional campaign and defeated her Republican opponent by 72.9% to 29.1%. No Republican has challenged her since and in 2008 she defeated a person who ran as No Party Affiliation by 77.5% to 22.5%. She is among the most liberal members of Congress, certainly an oddity in Florida. Nevertheless, she is extremely popular in her district.

District 21

The 21st district is another heavily Hispanic district located in Miami/Dade and Broward Counties. It has a Republican registration advantage, but most of them live in the Miami/Dade section of the district and outnumber the more Democratic sections that are located in Broward County. Seventy percent of the district is Hispanic, the highest of any district in the state. It has a R+5 PVI and should be fairly competitive.

That it has not been is something of a tribute to the incumbent Republican, Lincoln Diaz-Balart, the only person to hold the seat since its creation in 1992. Lincoln was born in Cuba and his aunt was the first wife of Fidel Castro. Over the years he has aggressively opposed Castro and hopes one day to return to Cuba. His has been somewhat liberal on economic issues and was one of only three Republicans who refused to sign Newt Ginrich's "Contract with America." Furthermore, he endeared himself to low income non-Hispanic residents in his district when he voted against the Republican welfare reform bills in 1996.

Diaz-Balart faced Democratic opposition only once between 1992 and 2006 and during this time he ran either unopposed or against a third party candidate. However, the district began to move towards the Democrats beginning in 2002–2004 and in 2006 he got his first challenge from a Democrat since 1996. Although he won by 59.5 % to 40.5%, the Democrats were emboldened and challenged him again in 2008, losing this time by 57.9% to 42.1%. Each time the Democrats ran a person with a Hispanic name and hope that in the future the slow change of the composition of the Hispanic population and its move to the Democratic Party will produce a winner in this district. The 2012 reapportionment will be especially crucial in this district.

District 22

Congressional District 22 stretches through two counties, Palm Beach and Broward, along the Atlantic coast of Florida. Starting in 1980 and continuing until 2006, the seat was held by Clay Shaw, a conservative Republican who had been the author of the forerunner of the 1996 Personal Responsibility Act and whose bill in 2004 to give workers the option of personal accounts over and above Social Security led to charges that he wanted to privatize Social Security.

As the Miami/Dade portion of his district became more Democratic and Shaw faced serious opposition from that Party, the Republican-dominated legislature in 2002 removed this section from the district. Nevertheless, the seat remained vulnerable and in March, 2005 state Senator Ron Klein announced he would run against Shaw in 2006 and within a month of the announcement raised $150,000. While Shaw was able to get close to Klein's finance totals in '06 ($4.7 million for Klein, $4.1 million for Shaw) Klein went on to win the seat by 50.9% to 47.1%, adding a second new seat in that year to the Democratic column.

In his freshman year in Congress, Klein was an active and visible member who was named "Rookie of the Year" by the news organization *The Politico*. The award cited his "willingness to cross party lines and his ability to get major legislation passed" as reasons for choosing him for the award. The Republicans apparently gave up on the seat and recruited Allen West, a retired African-American Army Lieutenant Colonel with no previous political experience who had only recently moved to the district, to run against Klein. They did little to help him. Klein raised nearly $4 million dollars for the race, while West raised about $600,000. Klein was re-elected by a margin of 54.7% to 45.3%.

District 23

This district is a majority black district that is "geographically contrived." It is located primarily in the Everglades, east and south of Lake Okeechobee. The constituents of the district range from upper middle class to working poor, with relatively few seniors. It has a large Haitian community. The Democrats have a 4 to 1 advantage in registration and it carries a D+28 PVI.

It has been represented since 1992 by Alcee Hastings, the only member of Congress ever to have been impeached and removed from office as a federal judge. After his impeachment and removal in 1989, he ran unsuccessfully for Governor in 1990 and then when the 23rd Congressional district was created, ran for that seat. He won the Democratic primary in a run-off and the general election by 59%-31% for the Republican. Since that time he has become Florida's most liberal Congressman and has won re-election often without opposition. He is noted for outstanding constituent relations and his website is depicted in English, Spanish and Creole. He won re-election in 2008 by 82% to 18% over his Republican opponent.

District 24

Florida District 24 was created in the 2002 reapportionment specifically for the sitting Republican Speaker of the Florida House of Representatives, Tom Feeney. It is located in Orange, Seminole, Volusia and Brevard Counties and is as close to a typical suburban district as Florida has. From its creation it had been in the hands of the Republicans, even though that Party had only a fourteen thousand person advantage in voter registration and the district carried an R+3 PVI.

In 2008, the incumbent was still Tom Feeney. A political powerhouse in Florida, Feeney had been the Speaker of the Florida House, Jeb Bush's first running mate for lieutenant governor of Florida and a confidante of President George W. Bush. He was once described by the *Washington Post* as the "Reaganest Republican."

Feeney was tainted by his links to disgraced lobbyist Jack Abramoff, was seen as one of the most vulnerable incumbents in the nation and the Democrats had challenged him in 2006. However, he escaped defeat when the Party put up a little-known and underfunded opponent.

The Democrats did not make that mistake in 2008. They recruited a widely respected former state representative, Suzanne Kosmas, and she won the Democratic primary, which Feeney tried to influence by spending money on robocalls in support of her opponent, Clint Curtis, who was thought to be the weaker of the two Democratic challengers. She then was backed by strong support from the Democratic Congressional Campaign Committee.

During the campaign, Kosmos made Feeney's ethical violations the central focus of her campaign and was able to keep pace with Fenney in fundraising

($2.10 million to $2.14 million). She won the election by a solid 16% margin, giving the Democrats a third new seat in Congress in 2008.

District 25

Congressional District 25 covers parts of three South Florida counties, Collier, Miami/Dade and Monroe. Including as it does the wild Everglades in Monroe County, it is geographically huge but its citizens are concentrated in a few population centers in the northern part of Miami/Dade (Hialeah Gardens, Tamiami, Kendale Lakes) in the farm town of Immokaalee in Collier County and in a number of small towns such as Shark, Mud Lake, and Squak Creek in the Ten Thousand Islands area along the Gulf Coast. It is a heavily Hispanic district, although the least Cuban of the three Hispanic Districts in Florida.

The incumbent Congressman is Mario Diaz-Balart, younger brother of twenty first district representative Lincoln Diaz-Balart. As chair of the 2002 Congressional Redistricting Committee in the Florida House of Representatives, Dias-Balart tailored this district for himself and won easily by 64.6% to 35.4% in 2002. He ran unopposed in 2004, but this district, like the other South Florida Hispanic districts had begun to change as immigrants from all around the nation and the world began to move in and the newer Cuban population became more interested in the economy and health care than in Fidel Castro. In addition Republican registration began to subside, and in 2004, the District was given a R+4 PVI, "leaning Republican," which gave the Democrats confidence that the right candidate could win the seat. They mounted a campaign in 2006, but did not raise enough money to be competitive and Diaz-Balart won by 58.5% to 41.5%.

In 2008, the Democrats recruited Joe Garcia, former executive director of the Cuban-American National Foundation and a local Democratic Party leader and provided him strong backing from national sources, including the addition of noted political strategist Joe Trippi, the former national campaign manager for Howard Dean, to his campaign staff. He was easily the most serious opponent Diaz-Balart had ever faced.

Garcia attacked Diaz-Balart for being out of touch with his constituency and for taking money from oil companies and for voting to give himself a pay raise, something that is automatically awarded by law. Diaz-Balart, who has always had a strong connection with his supporters, criticized Garcia for supporting a tax hike while a member of the State Public Service Commission and for cozying up to energy giant Enron.

Although Garcia was able to raise enough money to be competitive, ($1.7 million to $2.5 million) Diaz-Balart was able to fend him off and retain his seat by a margin of 53.1% to 46.9%, leaving the impression that the seat continued to be "in play."

INCUMBENCY SUCCESS

In American electoral campaigns, most incumbents win re-election when they try, and most win by substantial margins. This has been the case in Florida and around the nation, in congressional and other elections since the 1940's. Table 8.2 displays the data on this topic in U.S. and Florida congressional elections since the 1980's.

For virtually all of the time period involved, the two patterns look similar. Between 1990 and 2004, incumbents in Florida achieved an average re-election success rate of 98.4%. The rate at the national level was slightly lower, but still an impressive 94.9%. Furthermore, most other congressional elections in Florida were uncompetitive. Table 8.3 shows that eighty one percent of all congressional elections between 1982 and 2004 were classified as

Table 8.2. Incumbency Electoral Success, Florida and the Nation (1982–2008)

Year	Percent of Incumbents Re-Elected	
	Florida	*Nation*
1982	100%	90%
1984	100%	95%
1986	100%	98%
1988	94%	98%
1990	94%	96%
1992	100%	88%
1994	100%	90%
1996	100%	94%
1998	100%	98%
2000	100%	98%
2002	95%	96%
2004	100%	98%
2006	95%	94%
2008	88%	94%

Table 8.3. Competitiveness in Florida Congressional Elections (1982–2008)

	< 5%	5-10%	11-20%	21-40%	> 41%	Unopposed	Races with No Major Party Opposition
1982	1	1	3	5	6	3	0
1984	0	0	3	6	2	7	1
1986	0	0	0	3	7	7	2
1988	1	2	0	3	5	6	2
1990	2	0	5	4	2	5	1
1992	5	2	7	5	1	2	1
1994	1	1	3	6	1	7	4
1996	1	0	2	13	4	3	0
1998	0	0	1	4	1	15	2
2000	2	0	4	4	5	0	8
2002	1	1	2	8	4	6	3
2004	0	0	1	12	2	5	5
2006	3	1	7	8	0	5	1
2008	1	3	7	9	3	2	0

"landslides" by the Fair Vote *Index of Competitiveness*. That is, 81% of the elections were decided by a margin of 20% or higher.

In 2006 a break in this pattern appeared in Florida. In that year two incumbents in Florida were defeated (in both cases Democrats defeated Republicans) and the other Congressional races became more competitive. The landslide index dropped to 56%, indicating that only slightly more than one-half of the races were decided by margins of 20% or more. This was the second lowest rate since 1982.

In 2008, this pattern continued. More congressional incumbents were defeated in Florida in 2008 than in any other state: three. A Democrat defeated a Republican in both Districts 8 and 24 and a Republican defeated a Democrat in district 16. Thus the incumbency success rate was 88%, ten percentage points below the Florida average for the time period 1990–2006 and 6% below the national average for that period. Furthermore, the landslide index remained at 56%, suggesting that greater competition for Congressional seats in Florida may be in the offing.

EXPLAINING INCUMBENCY SUCCESS: CHALLENGER QUALITY AND CAMPAIGN SPENDING

Political incumbents are successful in their campaigns for re-election because they are more visible, more experienced at conducting campaigns and have greater financial resources. As a group, the incumbents in the Florida Congressional elections of 2008 possessed these characteristics and it was only in cases where the challenging parties recruited strong, experienced candidates who could generate the enthusiasm necessary to raise money and put into place a viable, professional campaign that incumbents were defeated. And in some cases, even these kinds of campaigns were not able to overcome incumbency advantage. In only seven Florida congressional districts were the kinds of challenger campaigns mounted in 2008 that could be expected to result in victories against incumbents. And only three of these were successful. These seven races took place in Districts 8, 13, 16, 18, 21, 24, and 25. They are examined in the following paragraphs.

Data in Table 8.4 shows how the average incumbent in the 2008 congressional campaigns in Florida swamped their opponents in fundraising, generating on average about $1.6 million compared to $400,000 for challengers, a margin of four to one. However, in the races that were seriously contested, incumbents were able to generate a much smaller margin of support, an average of $2.46 million to $1.98 million.

Table 8.4. Campaign Funds of Florida Congressional Candidates in 2008

Race	*Candidates*	*Amount Raised*
District 01	**Jeff Miller (R) ***	$360,055
	James Edward Bryan (D)	$13,784
District 02	**Allen Boyd (D) ***	$1,450,645
	Mark Mulligan (R)	$33,411
	Robert Ortiz (I)	$0
District 03	**Corrine Brown (D) ***	$559,627
District 04	**Ander Crenshaw (R) ***	$681,603
	James Joseph Mcgovern (D)	$170,557
District 05	**Ginny Brown-Waite (R) ***	$722,174
	John Timothy Russell (D)	$32,868
District 06	**Cliff Stearns (R) ***	$806,444
	Timothy M. Cunha (D)	$149,740
District 07	**John L. Mica (R) ***	$1,125,803
	Faye Armitage (D)	$32,929
District 08	Ric Keller (R) *	$1,619,406
	Alan Grayson (D)	$3,298,460
District 09	**Gus Bilirakis (R) ***	$1,494,533
	Bill Mitchell (D)	$277,009
	Richard Owings Emmons (3)	$38,015
	John Kalimnios (I)	$0
	Andrew Pasayan (I)	$0
District 10	**C. W. Bill Young (R) ***	$943,430
	Bob Hackworth (D)	$155,698
	Don Callahan (I)	$0
District 11	**Kathy Castor (D) ***	$631,095
	Eddie Adams (R)	$57,640

(continued)

Table 8.4. *(Continued)*

District 12	**Adam H. Putnam (R)** *	$1,843,688
	Doug Tudor (D)	$113,219
District 13	**Vernon Buchanan (R)** *	$4,374,205
	Christine Jennings (D)	$2,066,122
	Jan Schneider (I)	$18,209
	Don Baldauf (3)	$9,020
District 14	**Connie Mack (R)** *	$1,293,054
	Lawrence William Byrnes (I)	$53,879
	Jeffrey Peter George (I)	$20,326
	Robert M. Neeld, Jr. (D)	$15,781
	Burt Saunders (I)	$0
District 15	**Bill Posey (R)**	$944,893
	Steve Blythe (D)	$106,953
	Frank Zilaitis (3)	$45,743
District 16	Tim Mahoney (D) *	$3,034,464
	Tom Rooney (R)	$1,615,899
District 17	**Kendrick B. Meek (D)** *	$1,552,012
District 18	**Ileana Ros-Lehtinen (R)** *	$1,834,650
	Annette Taddeo (D)	$1,177,017
District 19	**Robert Wexler (D)** *	$2,908,098
	Ben Graber (I)	$271,032
	Edward J. Lynch (R)	$136,707
District 20	**Debbie Wasserman Schultz (D)** *	$1,721,750
	Margaret Hostetter (I)	$8,034
	Marc Luzietti (3)	$0
District 21	**Lincoln Diaz-Balart (R)** *	$2,284,221
	Raul L. Martinez (D)	$1,893,437
District 22	**Ron Klein (D)** *	$3,955,503
	Allen B. West (R)	$584,980
District 23	**Alcee L. Hastings (D)** *	$820,458

Table 8.4. *(Continued)*

	Marion Thorpe (R)	$42,185
	April Cook (I)	$0
District 24	Tom Feeney (R) *	$2,143,602
	Suzanne Kosmas (D)	$2,108,182
	Gaurav Bhola (I)	$6,725
District 25	**Mario Diaz-Balart (R) ***	$1,982,909
	Joe Garcia (D)	$1,787,665

The primary reason that the challengers in the seven "contested" races were able to raise the amount of money that they did was that they were "quality candidates" (Maisel, Stone and Maestas. 2000; Carson, Engstrom and Roberts. 2007) who possessed the kind of experience in government or politics or in business or professional pursuits that made large numbers of potential supporters believe that they could win a race for Congress. Tables 8.5 and 8.6 show general background differences between the more competitive candidates and those who were less competitive.

Two differences stand out. The first is that substantially more of the "serious" candidates had previously held substantial positions in government or public life and/or had run for public office than had the candidates who did less well. Several of the more successful candidates had contested in earlier years for the same office for which they were candidates in 2008. Nearly ninety percent (87.5%) of the candidates who ran close races had enjoyed the kind of highly visible, substantial experience in public life that makes one easily recognizable on the campaign trail and who give potential supporters reason to believe that they can be victorious in a campaign. In the non-competitive races, only 44% of the challengers had such experience.

The two groups also had different professional backgrounds. Almost all the serious candidates had emerged from those professions that throughout American history have been prominent in political and public life, attorneys and executives from the corporate or banking sectors. The less successful candidates came from different, and more diverse, backgrounds: 25% were retired from the military or from law enforcement; another 25% were small business owners or in the real estate business; and another 25% came from the "learned professions," college professors, medical doctors, engineers and the like. Empirical evidence suggests that candidates from all of the later backgrounds *can* be successful in public life, but this evidence also shows that voters may be biased towards law and business when making choices for public office because these professions appear to citizens to possess two important characteristics of a successful candidate, particular personal traits and campaign skills.

Table 8.5. Congressional Candidates Background and Experience, Competitive Races

District	Candidate		Challenger Notoriety			
			Political Experience	Occupation	Military Experience	Honors/Other
08	Ric Keller (R) *Incumbent					
	Alan Grayson (D)		Ran for this seat in 2006 and lost in the primary round	Attorney		Received national campaign attention and funding
13	**Vernon Buchanan (R) *Incumbent**					
	Christine Jennings (D)		Ran against Buchanan in 2006 and lost by 369 votes	Former bank president		
	Jan Schneider (I)		Previously ran as the district's Democratic nominee in 2002, 2004	Attorney		
	Don Baldauf (3)					
16	Tim Mahoney (D) *Incumbent					
	Tom Rooney (R)		Served as Assistant Attorney General in Florida	Attorney	Special Assistant U.S Attorney at Fort Hood, Taught law at WestPoint	
18	**Ileana Ros-Lehtinen (R) *Incumbent**					

	Annette Taddeo (D)		Held many various local political positions in Miami	Founder and CEO of large company		Named as one of the "Top 50 Latina Entrepreneurs" by Hispanic Magazine,
21	**Lincoln Diaz-Balart (R) *Incumbent**					
	Raul L. Martinez (D)		Former mayor and city council member of Hialeah (the district's largest city)			Hialeah City Hall is named after him
24	Tom Feeney (R) *Incumbent					
	Suzanne Kosmas (D)		Former Democratic State Representative	Small business owner		
	Gaurav Bhola (I)					
25	**Mario Diaz-Balart (R) *Incumbent**					
	Joe Garcia (D)		Appointed to the Florida Public Service Commission, Former Local party leader			Former director of the Cuban-American National Foundation

Table 8.6. Congressional Candidates Background and Experience, Non-Competitive Races

District	Candidate	Challenger Noteriety			
		Political & Campaign Experience	Occupation	Military Experience	Honors/Other
01	**Jeff Miller (R) *Incumbent**				
	James Edward Bryan (D)		Small business owner	Retired Army Sargent	
02	**Allen Boyd (D) * Incumbent**				
	Mark Mulligan (R)		Real estate developer		
	Robert Ortiz (I)		College Instructor		Named Fellow Visiting Scholar at the Claude Pepper Center at FSU
03	**Corrine Brown (D) *Incumbent**				
04	**Ander Crenshaw (R) *Incumbent**				
	James Joseph "Jay" McGovern (D)	Chairman of various development and preservation organizations in Jacksonville	Engineer	Retired Navy Pilot	
05	**Ginny Brown-Waite (R) *Incumbent**				
	John Timothy Russell (D)	Ran for this seat twice before, and lost in the primary round both times	Nurse		
06	**Cliff Stearns (R) *Incumbent**				

	Timothy M. Cunha (D)	Served in many public and party offices (but all were in New Jersey)	Attorney		
07	**John L. Mica (R) *Incumbent**				
	Faye Armitage (D)	Stem cell research activist	Former professor of economics		
09	**Gus Bilirakis (R) *Incumbent**				
	Bill Mitchell (D)	Ran for State House in District 47 in 2002 (as a Republican) and lost.	Attorney and founder of large law group	Vietnam veteran	
	Richard Owings Emmons (3)		Small business owner		
	John Kalimnios (I)		Retired police officer		
	Andrew Pasayan (I)				
10	**C. W. Bill Young (R) *Incumbent**				
	Bob Hackworth (D)	Former mayor and city commissioner of Dunedin	Textbook publisher		
	Don Callahan (I)				
11	**Kathy Castor (D) *Incumbent**				
	Eddie Adams (R)	Ran for this seat in 2006 and lost	Small business owner		
12	**Adam H. Putnam (R) *Incumbent**				

(continued)

Table 8.6. *(Continued)*

	Doug Tudor (D)	Secretary of the FL Democratic Party's Veterans' Caucus		Retired Navy	
14	**Connie Mack (R) *Incumbent**				
	Lawrence William Byrnes (I)		College professor		
	Jeffrey Peter George (I)			Retired Army	
	Robert M. Neeld Jr. (D)		Accountant		
	Burt Saunders (I)	Former State Senator	Attorney		
15	**Bill Posey (R)**	Former State Senator and State House Rep.	Real estate		
	Steve Blythe (D)		Medical doctor		
	Frank Zilaitis (3)		Attorney		
17	**Kendrick B. Meek (D) *Incumbent**				
19	**Robert Wexler (D) *Incumbent**				
	Ben Graber (I)	Former representative in the FL House, former mayor of Broward County	Medical doctor		
	Edward J. Lynch (R)		Small business owner		
20	**Debbie Wasserman Schultz (D) *Incumbent**				

	Margaret Hostetter (I)		Ran for this seat in 2004 and lost, Member of many municipal civic committees	Real estate agent and business owner		
	Marc Luzietti (3)		Secretary of the Socialist Party of Florida			
22	**Ron Klein (D) *Incumbent**					
	Allen B. West (R)				Retired Army Lieutenant Colonel	In 2004, the conservative *Frontpage* Magazine named him "Man of the Year"
23	**Alcee L. Hastings (D) *Incumbent**					
	Marion Thorpe (R)		Worked in the Agency for Health Care Administration State of Florida, former delegate at the RNC			
	April Cook (I)					

SUMMARY

As the 2008 campaign season began, political analysts defined Florida as a "battle ground" state at the presidential level and others put nine (9) congressional districts in the category of "at risk" for the incumbent. These districts included 2 Democratic seats (16 and 22) and 7 Republican (8, 13, 15, 18, 21, 24 and 25). The potential for major change in the Florida congressional delegation was clearly present.

Given these prognostications, the outcome of the campaign was somewhat anti-climatic. Despite the Democratic victory in the presidential race, the Democrats picked up only two Congressional seats, but lost one themselves, leaving the distribution at 15 Republicans to 10 Democrats, a net increase of one Democrat over the 2006 numbers. Furthermore, most of the twenty-five races were non-competitive. If a margin of victory of 55%–45% or less is used as a measure of a competitive election, then there were only four competitive congressional races (19%) in Florida in 2008.

The campaign of Barack Obama had little impact on the outcome of the Congressional election. While he ran ahead of Democrats in 16 of the 25 congressional races and was even with the Democratic candidate in one other, he was unable to influence the result. He ran behind all but one of the winning candidates and in this one exception, the congressional winner got 82% of the vote and Obama got 83%, hardly a game-changing margin. In the races in which Democratic candidates lost, they did so even though Obama got more votes than they did. He was unable to transfer his vote to them and did not win enough "extra" votes to make a difference anyway. The presidential and congressional campaigns in Florida in 2008 appear to have been run in parallel but separate universes.

Given the partisan composition of the state—with Democrats in a sizeable majority—much of the absence of competitiveness can be attributed to the apportionment plan adopted in 2002. The next opportunity to address the inequities involved in this plan will be the state legislative elections of 2010. The following section discusses the context of those elections.

Part IV

THE STATE LEGISLATIVE RACES

Chapter Nine

The Outcome of the 2008 Election Cycle

INTRODUCTION

In addition to the presidential race and the twenty-five congressional races, Floridians in 2008 were slated to go to the polls in one hundred and twenty state House districts and twenty-one of Florida's forty state Senate districts. While the Democrats' enjoyed a seemingly blue state 41%-to-37% edge over Republicans in voter registration in 2008, it was the Republicans who controlled two-thirds of the legislature.

Both the Florida State Senate and the Florida House districts are organized by population. Although there are exactly three times as many members of the House (120) as in the Senate (40), the Senate's political boundaries are independent and do not consist of three House districts. In Florida, state House members are elected to two-year terms during even-numbered years. Once elected, members are term limited to four consecutive terms. However, they can run again after a two year absence.

State Senators in even-numbered districts are elected along with the elections for Florida's statewide offices in years ending in the digit 2. Senators in odd-numbered districts are elected in years divisible by four, U.S. Presidential elections years. Due to redistricting, in years ending in the digit 2, all Senate Districts are up for re-election. Therefore following the 2001 redistricting, odd-number district Senators were elected to two-year terms in 2002, and even-number district Senators will be elected to two-year terms in 2012. Once elected, members are limited to two consecutive terms.

As was the case with regard to the U.S. Congress, the Florida State Legislature was dominated by Democrats throughout much of the 20th century and it was not until 1990 when the Republicans gained a tie in the State Senate that the Republicans began to turn their electoral gains in the national elections to their advantage in the State Legislature. The data are shown in Table 9.1. In 1992, Republicans gained control of the State Senate, and in 1996 with their takeover of the State House of Representatives, Florida became one of the first legislatures in the former confederacy to fall under complete GOP control.

The Republicans quickly took advantage of their new position of power and in the reapportionment plan following the 2000 census re-organized district lines to their advantage. In the aftermath of that session, Republicans have dominated both the House and the Senate and the level of competition in these two bodies decreased immediately as a function of districts drawn in such a way as to make almost all "safe." Data provided by Kevin Wagner and Eric Prior (2008; 173) illustrate this phenomenon. Their analysis shows that the percentage of candidates for House of Representatives who ran unopposed "shot up" from 12 percent in 2000 to 43 percent in 2004 and the percentage of State Senators who ran unopposed increased from 38% to 50% in 2006. By 2002, Republicans had gained control of the State House by a margin of 79 to 41 and of the Senate by 26 to 14.

Table 9.1. Distribution of Legislative Seats in Florida by Political Party (1980–2006)

	Florida Senate		**Florida House of Representatives**	
	Republicans	Democrats	Republicans	Democrats
1980	12	28	39	81
1982	9	31	36	84
1984	8	32	43	77
1986	14	26	45	75
1988	16	24	46	74
1990	16	24	46	74
1992	20	20	49	71
1994	21	19	57	63
1996	23	17	62	58
1998	23	17	70	50
2000	25	15	75	45
2002	26	14	79	41
2004	26	14	82	38
2006	26	14	78	42
2008	26	14	76	44

The full benefits of gerrymandering came to the Republicans in 2004 when they gained an additional 3 seats in the House and lost no incumbents who sought re-election. In addition, 60 seats were unopposed, only 5% of the 120 House seats had vote margins of less than 10%, and 67.5% had margins of 21% or greater. Since then, the Democrats have fought to regain ground they lost in the aftermath of that election.

In 2006, the Democrats finally began to regain ground. In that year they engineered an overall gain of four seats in the House, their first gains in fourteen years. In the Senate in that year, each party won one of the other party's seats. Alachua County Sheriff Steve Oelrich captured the reliably Democratic District 14 for the Republicans and State Representative Charlie Justice took advantage of a bruising GOP primary and the shifting demographists of Pinellas County to deliver a previously Republican seat for the Democrats.

As the 2008 Presidential electoral season opened, Republicans held a 78-42 majority in the House and a 26-14 majority in the Senate. However, based on the 2006 results, it appeared that additional Democratic gains might be on the horizon. In June of 2008, Steve Schale, to whom the Democratic Party gave the task of electing Democrats to the Florida House observed that "It used to be five or six battleground districts in play each election cycle. I'm not sure you can say it's only five or six now. There could be 20 or 25. A lot of places are going to be in play," (FL Trend 6/1/08).

OUTCOME

As was the case in the Congressional races, the great excitement created by the Obama campaign and the sophisticated, well-funded voter identification and turnout efforts designed and employed by the Democrats did not trickle down to the legislative campaigns. President Obama carried 20 State Senate districts (half of all districts) and 55 (45% of all districts) State House districts, but when the polls closed, the 2008 Florida legislative elections were characterized by a lack of competition resulting in a lack of change.

The election produced a net gain of one seat by the Democrats in the House of Representatives and no change in the Senate. Only one of 81 incumbents lost his or her seat, 35% of the House districts and 29% of the Senate districts sent legislators to represent them in Tallahassee without a single general election vote (they were unopposed and therefore did not appear on the ballot), and 52% of the House seats and 48% of the Senate seats did not have candidates of both major parties in the races. More than one half of the State House seats either had no contests or were decided by margins of 40% or greater and more than 60% of the races in the House and 66% in the Senate were decided by margins of 21% or greater. Fewer than 15% of Florida House seats and fewer than 5% of Florida Senate seats were decided by margins of 10% or less, the traditional gauge of a competitive election.

EXPLAINING NON-COMPETITIVENESS: THE COCKTAIL OF APPORTIONMENT, INCUMBENCY, AND TERM LIMITS

Given the unique redistricting of 2002, some observers of Florida politics assume that the 2008 outcomes can be traced solely to mal-apportionment and "safe" seats. Legislative apportionment was clearly a significant part of the story, but the absence of competition in 2008 can also be linked to two other factors: incumbency and term limits. These variables worked in combination to diminish competition and the prospect of significant Florida electoral realignment.

The Apportionment Process

Apportionment and reapportionment are designed to ensure that each voter is equally represented by Florida and federal legislators. Reapportionment in Florida generally happens every ten years following the national census. Based on U.S. Supreme Court decisions, the districts must be practically equal in population and must be contiguous. From a political perspective the process allows the party in control in the legislature great influence over the results, which ultimately provides an advantage to that party in the electoral process.

For years, the Florida legislature under the control of conservative Democrats maintained one of the most egregiously mal-apportioned representational systems in the nation. During the 1960's fewer than 20 percent of Florida voters were able to elect a majority in both chambers of the white male dominated Florida legislature. After federal court intervention and a new constitution in the late 1960's, legislative seats were redrawn in a more balanced way. Further evolution occurred when the NAACP and the Republican Party of Florida formed an alliance to create minority districts in the 1970's and 1980's, the beginning of a mutually beneficial alliance. The alliance succeeded in eliminating multi-member districts which had been designed to elect entrenched white Democrats. These districts were replaced with single member districts, a number of which were created specifically to give an advantage to black candidates. For the Republicans the alliance worked because in addition to eliminating Democrat incumbents by combining their districts into heavily black districts, bordering districts were "bleached" and became more complementary to Republican candidates. As the Chair of the Republican Party put it in 2002, "the creation of every black Democratic district creates two Republican districts." (Bridges. 2002)

By 2002, the Republican's legislative majorities gave them control of the apportionment process for the first time and they set out to maximize their advantage. Their efforts were aided by the implementation of legislative term limits which had been approved by Florida voters in 1992. The effect of these limits was first seen in the 2002 session and had an unintended consequence, small numbers of incumbents to protect in redistricting. This provided the Republicans, as the party in control of the redistricting process in that year, the luxury of drawing new legislative boundaries with little regard to saving the seats of individual members. They took advantage of this opportunity to maximize safe seats and to build their majorities. They did so by drawing districts that were "far more likely to include Cuban-Hispanics rather than non-Cuban Hispanics in Hispanic-majority districts" and by "fragmenting and packing Democratic voters into House and Senate districts" so that "with less than 50% of the average vote across all districts, Republicans win a majority of the vote in two-thirds of all districts and Democrats win in one third." (Lichtman, 2002. 30; 2) The likely outcomes in 2004 were transparent enough that they were predicted almost precisely in advance of the election. Professor Alan Lichtman at American University estimated prior to the election that Republicans would win eighty-two House seats (they won 81), twenty six state Senate seats (they won twenty six), and eighteen seats in the U.S. Congress (they won 18). In the aftermath of the reapportionment plan the Republican Party Chair said "now, as far as the eye can see, Republicans will control both houses in Florida." (Bridges) While the Democrats in 2006 made some adjustments to the apportionment carried out in 2002, the 2008 legislative districting characteristics in Florida continued to reflect a decidedly pro-Republican bias.

Incumbency

As is the case with Congressional candidates, state legislators who run for re-election more often than not are re-elected. Incumbents have several structural advantages over challengers, including name recognition, fundraising and the trappings of the elected office. Incumbents typically have run previous campaigns, either against minor party or write-in candidates or against major party opposition; these campaigns allow incumbents to increase their name recognition and to hone their campaign strategies and techniques. They normally have access to a pool of political action committee and corporate contributions and, especially in the case of the Republicans in Florida, to party support. Thus, they are usually much better financed than are any rivals.

Finally, they can rely on their legislative office to send out press releases and taxpayer financed district newsletters, a huge asset in low visibility races such as state legislative campaigns. These assets make them difficult targets for small opposition campaigns to overcome.

Term Limits

Term limits were added to the Florida Constitution by a citizen initiative in 1992 that was supported by 77% of the voters. As a result, Florida state legislators are limited to no more than eight consecutive years in office. The provision took effect with the 2000 election, making 55 representatives and 11 senators ineligible to run for re-election in 2002, a major boon to Republican efforts to re-draw the district lines. For the first time in Florida history, the party in power had few incumbents to feed during the redistricting food fight and as a result, the Republican Party was given considerable latitude in drawing a map favorable to maintaining and building up its legislative majorities.

As time moved forward, term limits continued to influence legislative races. Aware that there will be a near-term opportunity to run for a seat in which there is no incumbent, potential challengers often wait for these incumbents to retire rather than take them on directly. As a result, competition for legislative seats is depressed.

THE EFFECTS OF THE COCKTAIL IN THE 2008 LEGISLATIVE CAMPAIGNS

As was the case with the Congressional elections in Florida, very few of those for the state legislature were decided by activities related to the candidates or the campaigns involved. That is, the traditional determinants of campaign outcomes, message, money and mechanics, were subsumed under the weight of apportionment, incumbency and term limits. The vast majority of the outcomes in the 2008 Florida legislative elections can be explained either by one, or a combination of, these three variables. Using the most generous definitions, only 18 of the 120 House seats and one of the 20 Senate seats can be said to have been determined during or by the activities involved in the 2008 campaigns.

The Effects of Apportionment upon Competition

The favorable legislative map that the Republicans drew in 2002 packed Democratic voters into as few districts as possible, effectively ensuring that many of the remaining seats would be safe for their own candidates. The effect of this strategy lingered throughout the ensuing years. In 2008, over 90% of the districts that were drawn in 2002 elected representatives from the same party as they did in that first year after reapportionment.

In 2008, 32% of state House districts had a registration advantage for one party or the other of 20% or more and 45.8% had such advantages of 11% or greater. In the Senate, the numbers were 40% and 60% respectively. The results were predictable: facing odds stacked against them, potential candidates opted not to run for office. Thus, in 2008 forty four (44) legislators ran unopposed and 21 ran in districts in which the races were decided by electoral margins of 40% or greater. Outcomes such as these suggest the absence of a competitive environment, and over 60% of those who ran unopposed had registration advantages of +10% or greater for one party or the other. And 75% (21of 28) of those who won by 40% or greater had such an advantage. Clearly, the manner in which legislative district boundaries were drawn in 2002 influenced the outcome of 2008 legislative races.

The Effect of Incumbency upon Competition

In 2008, 67 incumbents ran for seats in the Florida House of Representatives and 14 ran for seats in the Senate. Only one of these individuals, Democratic representative Tony Sasso in House District 32, lost his race and he had won the seat only a year earlier in a Republican district that the Democrats won on a fluke. In addition, only 10 of the 67 House incumbents and one of the 14 Senate incumbents were involved in races that meet the usual standard of competitiveness in American politics, victory margins of 10% or less. In short, if you are an incumbent Florida state legislator you are almost guaranteed re-election.

As suggested earlier, incumbency brings substantial benefits to a candidate, not the least of which is financial advantage. In 2008, incumbents in the House raised, on average, more than twice the amount of money as did their opponents, $160,474 to $63,328 for challengers. In the Senate the margin was about 7 to 1 and the comparable figures were $531,342 and $73,974. Republican incumbents held a particular advantage in fundraising, gathering an average of $670,672 to as opposed to $231,950 by their Democratic counterparts in the Senate and by raising an average of $190,865 to $105,432 in the House.

The Effects of Term Limits Upon Competition

In 2008 roughly 30% of the incumbent House seats that did not appear on the ballot due to lack of competition and 33% of the commensurate Senate seats were defined by voter registration figures as competitive districts. Evidence suggests that potential challengers in these races were simply waiting until the incumbent left office, rather than taking on a potentially expensive campaign. Incumbency in such circumstances is preventing opposition party challenges in even the most attractive seats. We suspect that once these members are term limited, these seats will become battleground seats, with the potential to be won by the "out" party. Open Florida Senate seats saw major party opposition at a rate almost double the rate of incumbents without immediate term limits. On the House side, term limited open incumbent seats were almost three times more likely than "normal" or non-term limited incumbents to see major party challengers in 2008. An additional 41% of open House seats and 50% of open Senate seats had contested primaries in 2008; conversely 3% of incumbent House members and no incumbent Florida senators faced primary challengers.

MINOR PARTY CANDIDATES

A notable feature of legislative elections in Florida is the relatively high number of minor party candidates who file, despite the fact that no write-in or minor party candidate has ever won a Florida legislative race. In the run up to the 2008 elections, 30 Florida House districts (25%) and 6 Florida Senate districts (28.5%) had minor party or write-in candidates, giving the appearance of competition.

While these candidates might be the product of a rising independent movement in the State, recent history suggests that this is not the case. Instead, they are the product of a not-so-secret dirty secret in Florida politics: political operatives employ minor party and/or write-in candidates to achieve a variety of campaign objectives. In many instances, these candidates are recruited to allow unopposed major party candidates to raise money and run a campaign in an effort to raise positive name identification for political endeavors after terming out, including a later run for a Florida Senate or Congressional seat. In other cases, they are recruited to drain votes from the opposition party in competitive seats. Typically Green Party candidates are recruited to take votes from Democrats and Libertarian or TEA Party candidates are used to siphon votes from Republican candidates. Our evidence suggests that this was the case in 20 of the 30 House districts and 4 of the 6 Senate districts with write-in or minor party opposition.

Florida is a closed primary state unless there is no opposition in the general election, when voters of any party can participate in the primary of the dominant party. Thus a major factor stimulating minor parties and write-in candidates is

Democratic and Republican Party recruitment of candidates to file as write-in candidates in the general election in order to ensure that their own primary is closed, thus preventing opposition party voters from playing a role in choosing the nominee. We suggest this is the case in 10 of the 30 House districts and 2 of the 6 Senate districts with write-in or minor party opposition, since these races also featured general election candidates from the major parties.

In an effort to address what many activists saw as a loophole regarding write-in candidates, *Jacobson v. Martin, Lake Co. Circuit Court, 2006-ca-1160* was filed arguing that such candidates in general elections are not legitimate and therefore should be deemed not to exist. The court ruled that a write-in candidate is "opposition" and should not be treated as non-existent. Nevertheless, for purposes of describing legislative competition in Florida, we place these seats in the unopposed category, as a write-in or minority candidate has never won in Florida. This placement brings the number of unopposed Florida House seats in 2008 to 62 or over one-half and in the Senate to 10, almost half. Our data indicates that this absence of competition is linked to the interrelationship of apportionment, incumbency and term limits.

TIGHT LEGISLATIVE RACES

The foregoing analysis described the outcome of two kinds of Florida legislative races: 1) those that did not appear on the November 2008 ballot and 2) those that were on the ballot with only token opposition. We are left with half of the Florida House races and nearly half of the Florida Senate races featuring candidates from both major parties. In this section we turn our attention to these seats, the 48% of Florida House seats and 52 % of Florida Senate seats that had candidates from both major parties on the November ballot.

Of the 58 House seats with major parties squaring off, roughly one-third (18) ended up being decided by electoral margins of 10% or less. There was substantially less competition on the Senate side with one of the eleven being decided by 10% or less. Each of these races has a different set of dynamics and circumstances, but the general rule is that the candidates and parties typically invest their resources in a handful of battleground seats because they believe they have the opportunity to win under the existing demographic circumstances. However, districts are not always what they may demographically appear to be and on occasion higher level agendas drive the competition. To illustrate the forces that influenced the outcome of competitive races in Florida, we first provide vignettes of the tight legislative races, those decided by 5% or less. Subsequently, we provide a brief overview of the competitive seats, those decided by more than 5% and less than 10%.

The 2008 Florida legislative elections ultimately saw 11 House races and one Senate race with a margin of victory of 5% or less. Following the election, 4 of the 11 House seats are held by the "opposition" party as defined by voter registration. Of the eleven tight seats, two changed sides of the aisle, one from Republican to Democrat and one from Democrat to Republican. Overall, the Democrats picked up a net of one legislative seat in 2008. Of the eleven tight races five were term limited open seats. The Senate race was an anomaly as it occurred in a "safe" district under a unique set of circumstances. Following is a brief discussion of these races.

In assessing the outcomes of these races we discovered that voter registration data does not fully explain the true potential for competition in the legislature races because a large number of Floridians do not vote along party lines, particularly in down ballot races. Therefore we have created a relatively simple "generic" district performance formula, designed to better comprehend the landscape of each legislative district. It is analogous to the Cook Partisan Voting Index utilized in our analysis of the Congressional races.

This generic performance number is arrived at by calculating the difference in district level electoral results for the highest performing statewide candidates from each party during the most recent previous elections. The differences are displayed in Appendix 1 and help explain the outcomes of the legislative races. For example, House District 11 has a Democratic voter registration advantage of 16.2 %. However, the difference between the two highest performing state level candidates in the 2008 elections showed an 8.8% Republican margin. In that year the incumbent Democrat won the district by only .02% while outspending the Republican by more than $60,000. While these figures are suggestive rather than definitive, they are useful in predicting the outcomes of state legislative races. Nevertheless, once the influence of apportionment, incumbency and term limits are factored in, competition declines.

HD 3 is one of three Democrat voter registration advantage seats in the Central North Florida area that were competitive. Geographically, district 3 lies in a part of the Florida that has been dubbed LA or lower Alabama. The district encompasses nearly all of the cities of Pensacola and Gulf Breeze. District 3 enjoys a Democratic registration advantage of + 6.7%. However, it has been a Republican seat since 2000, when former Representative Holly Benson became the first Republican ever elected. Although a Democrat seat by registration, from a generic performance perspective the seat is R+ 7.16. Incumbent Republican Clay Ford was able to carry the district by 4.2%, outspending his opposition nearly four to one.

HD 9 Geographically district 9 resides in the Northwestern corner of Jefferson County and in the northern portion Leon County. The district encompasses a large portion of Florida's capital city of Tallahassee and is home to many State of Florida employees and Florida State football fans. The district enjoys a Democratic voter registration advantage of 17.4%, has a sizeable African American population and has been reliably Democratic since the civil war. Following the 2000 redistricting, Democrat Lorrane Ausley was elected to four consecutive terms. With Ausley term limited, the Republicans found a dream candidate in former NFL All Pro and Florida State All American Football star Peter Boulware, an African American. The Republicans saw the Boulware candidacy as an opportunity to make the Democrats focus energy on a safe seat, putting them on defense and diverting their attention from building upon their electoral gains of 2006. Boulware faced off against Michelle Rehwinkle Vasilinda who ultimately beat him by 430 votes, despite being outspent $485,641 to $194,377.

HD 11 Geographically, district 11 is a wide ranging rural district including all of Gilchrist, Lafayette and Suwannee Counties. The district is one of the 31 districts carried by both the top performing statewide Democratic candidate, CFO Alex Sink, and the top performing statewide Republican, Governor Charlie Crist. District 11 appears to be a safe Democratic seat with a 16.2 % Democratic voter registration advantage. Affirming this, the voters had elected Democrat Dwight Stanzel to consecutive terms prior to redistricting through terming out in 2006. Again in HD 11, the Republicans saw an opportunity to make the Democrats focus on a relatively safe seat. Although not as safe as the open HD 9, the seat was held by a Democrat Incumbent, Debbie Boyd. As Boyd, a sixth generation Floridian, looked to defend her seat, the generic performance data (+8.8 R) showed the race had the potential to be substantially more competitive than voter registration data suggested. In an effort to identify with her constituents Boyd proudly recalled that as a young girl, she took tobacco off for a half penny per stick. She ended up outspending her Republican opponent, Elizabeth Porter by $206,412 to $145, 116 and squeaking past Porter by .02% in a recount.

HD 21 This wide ranging district encompasses all of Putnam County along with portions of Clay, Marion, Lake and Volusia Counties. Although represented by Republican Joe Pickens until terming out in 2008, district 21 voter registrations is D + 8.3. However, the District's generic performance is R +13.6. Given that Pickens was term limited in 2008, both parties viewed this as a battleground seat. Coming out of the primary, the GOP leadership's chosen candidate faltered and little known architect Steve Van Zant emerged as the Republican nominee. On the Democrat side, Linda Myers, a conservative local business woman and former Putnam County Commissioner ran unopposed. When the polls closed in the general election, the little known Republican Van Zant was able to keep the seat in Republican hands edging out Myers by 3% despite being slightly outspent by her $140,681 to $131,540.

HD 32 This district includes portions of Brevard and Orange Counties and is one of the 31 House districts carried by both the top performing statewide Democratic and Republican candidates. The seat had been held by Republican Bob Allen since 2000. Allen made national headlines in 2007 after being arrested for offering $20 for the privilege of performing oral sex on an undercover male police officer in a public park. Despite having a R+ 5.90 registration, following Allen's arrest Democrat Tony Sasso took the seat for the Democrats in a special election to replace Allen. The Republican party recruited agribusiness man Steve Crisafulli to challenge the incumbent Sasso in 2008. Crisafulli was able to flip the seat back to a Republican seat; beating Sasso by 4.4%.This was the one instance in 2008 that an incumbent lost.

HD 40 Geographically, the district resides entirely in Orange county and Southeastern portion of the greater Orlando area. This district was located in the portion of one of the four counties that the Obama campaign was able to flip from 2004. The district is also one of the 31 districts carried by both the Democratic candidate, CFO Alex Sink and the Republican, Governor Charlie Crist. The district voter registration is R + 1.40% and the performance is R +8.89%. The district was an open seat in 2008 as term limited incumbent Andy Gardner who was elected in 2000 by 9% was running for the Florida Senate. After a difficult Republican primary, Republican attorney Eric Eisnaugle defeated Democrat Todd Christian by 5% in the General Election, keeping the seat in the Republican column.

HD 48 Geographically, the district lies almost entirely in northern Pinellas County and includes Tarpon Springs, Palm Harbor and a portion of Clearwater. The district is one of the 31 districts carried by both the top performing Democratic and Republican candidates and part of one of the four counties that flipped from Republican to Democratic in 2008. The registration was R +11%, however the performance was R +6.38%, suggesting a more competitive seat. In this race, specific candidate characteristics came into placy and after a bruising race and some awkward personal financial revelations, incumbent Republican Peter Nehr was re-elected by 2% of the vote, having outspent his opponent $287,178 to $74,846.

HD 65 This district resides entirely in Polk County. The seat is one of the 31 districts carried by both the two top performing Democratic and Republican candidates. The seat has a voter registration advantage of D +8 and a contrasting performance of R +4.9. Although registration data suggests a Democrat seat, the seat had been held by Republican Marty Bowen who had first won election in 2000, beating her Democrat challenger by 7.6%. With Bowen terming out, the race for the open seat featured Republican Realtor John Wood and Democratic research chemist Bob Hagenmaier. Wood was able to defeat Hagenmaier by 3.6%, outspending him $187,892 to $14,400.

The financial disparity in this open seat appears to be, in part, a result of the Democratic leadership being focused upon defending HDs 9 and 11.

HD 69 Geographically, the district contains the city of Sarasota and part of Manatee County. The district is another of the 31 House districts carried by both the top performing statewide Democratic candidate and Republican candidates. The voter registration is D+7.5, however the performance is a more competitive D +1.89. The seat had been held by Republican Donna Clarke who had initially won election in 2000 by 3.6%. The 2008 race was a rematch of the 2006 open seat contest where Democrat Peter Fitzgerald narrowly defeated Republican Laura Benson 51% to 49% switching a Republican seat to Democrat. With rumors circulating that Benson had previously been a pole dancer, she was less successful than in 2006 as incumbent Fitzgerald improved his margin to 4.3% after out spending her $258,066 to $157,150.

HD 81 Geographically, the district covers portions of Martin and St. Lucie counties. Republican term limited Gayle Harrell was elected in 2000 beating her Democratic opponent by 17.8%. The open seat had a much more competitive voter registration of R +1.8 and a performance R +3.97. Much like in HD 21 the GOP leadership's chosen candidate faltered. However, the story would end differently in the treasure coast as allegations swirled that Republican County Commission Michael DiTerlizzi had voted to increase gasoline taxes by 50 percent and then, as a gas station owner, began selling gas to the county. Despite being outspent by DiTerlizzi, $275,695 to $ 177,011, Democrat Adam Fetterman was able to put the seat in the Democrat column, winning by 4.9%. This victory offset the Republican win in HD 32.

HD 83 From a geographic perspective, House District 83 is located entirely within Palm Beach County lines. The district registration is R + 8.4, however the performance is D +.57. Representative Carl Domino won a four-way primary in the 2002 GOP Primary with 31.09% of the vote and went on to win the general election. He was unopposed in subsequent primary elections and won each general election since, the closest being the 2006 general election where he scraped by challenger Rick Ford winning by 627 votes with 50.6% of the vote. Domino suggested the small margin in 2006 was due to fall-out from the Mark Foley cybersex scandal, which is plausible given that their districts overlapped. The Democratic Party was able to recruit a rising party star, attorney and Obama-activist Brian Miller to post up against Domino. Miller was able to practically match the incumbent dollar for dollar, raising $248,245 to Domino's $258,356. While Miller worked nights and weekends knocking on doors and canvassing, Representative Domino boldly predicted he did not have to spend his time campaigning because, "the rich people on the east side of the district are going to vote for me. I've been in office six years. People know what I stand for." He proved prophetic and won re-election by 4 points.

SD 19. Senate District 19 was the lone tight Florida Senate race. The district is in Orange and Osceola Counties, both counties that flipped from Republican to Democratic in 2008. Voter Registration in the District is D+ 36.2 % and the performance is D +25.13%. When the district was drawn, it was clearly created as an extremely safe Democrat seat. However, incumbent Senator Gary Siplin made the seat competitive in 2008 when he was convicted for using the services of Florida employees for his candidacy. The matter had been confined to the halls of Tallahassee until a local television camera crew aired footage of Siplin wearing his Sunday best, jumping a barbed wire fence in an effort to avoid discussing his conviction on camera. Ironically, while able to vote from his elected office, as a convicted felon Siplin could not vote in elections. In an attempt to rectify this he sponsored legislation that would restore voting rights to fellow convicted felons. Ultimately, incumbent Senator Siplin squeaked by challenger Belinda Ortiz by 1% in a very safe district during a presidential election. This race is an anomaly given that Siplin outspent Ortiz by more than two to one to win by 1% in a district that favored his party by a substantial margin.

In addition to the eleven tight races described above, there were eight House races in 2008 that were decided by margins greater than 5%, but less than 10%; no Florida Senate races fell into this category. Following the election, three of these eight House seats were held by the "opposition" party as defined by voter registration and 66% of these were incumbents prior to 2008. Demonstrating the lack of change in Florida electoral politics, only one of the eight competitive seats (District 10) switched sides of the aisle from Republican to Democrat. And this seat was held by a term limited Republican who had been elected originally as a Democrat and subsequently switched parties. This win resulted in the Democrats picking up a net of one seat in the Florida House. These data further underscore the effects of the cocktail upon the Florida legislative electoral process; 62% of the eight competitive races were open seats.

Part V

FLORIDA ELECTIONS OF 2008 IN PERSPECTIVE

Chapter Ten

The 2008 Elections and the Future of Florida Politics

The outcomes of the Florida elections of 2008 exhibited change at the Presidential level and continuity at the Congressional and State Legislative levels. These outcomes were heavily influenced by four factors: changing demographics in the state, a shift in attitudes among the baby boomer generation, Barack Obama's superiority in "money, message and mechanics," (Crew, Bayliss and Moore. 2010) and the apportionment of the US Congress and the Florida State Legislature. Several of these factors will continue to play a role in the elections of 2010 and beyond.

Throughout the state's history, demographic changes have played a major role in Florida politics, contributing especially to the rise of the Republican Party and to the increasing conservatism of that Party. In 2008, demographic trends began to favor the Democrats and may continue to do so. Especially important in the presidential race was the overall increase in the non-Cuban Hispanic population and the resulting changes in the populations in the three traditionally Hispanic Congressional districts and in the "Disney district," number eight in central Florida.

The 2008 election was the first in which non-Cuban Hispanics outnumbered Cubans. These populations, from Mexico, Central America and especially Puerto Rico, are more likely to side with Democratic than Republican candidates and their support of Barack Obama was crucial in his victory. Their numbers are also increasing while the Cuban Hispanic numbers are declining. To the extent to which this group of voters maintains its favor for state-wide Democratic candidates, this party will prosper in future presidential elections.

This group of voters is also likely to have an influence on four congressional districts in 2010; number 8 which includes Orange and the surrounding counties that make up a large portion of the workforce for Disney World and the three historically Hispanic congressional districts, 18, 21 and 25. In District 8, a combination of increasing numbers of Puerto Ricans, African-Americans and working class voters into the Orange County portion of the district has made it, once safe for Republicans, into one where strong Democrats can be expected to win.

Assuming that the "new" Hispanics move to the existing Hispanic neighborhoods in Florida, and continue to vote Democratic, partisan dynamics are also likely to be affected in Congressional Districts, 18, 21 and 25. The incumbent Republican Cuban-American in district 25 resigned in the summer of 2010 and his brother who represented district 21 resigned his seat in order to shift to number 25, making both seats "open." These changes are already encouraging strong non-Cuban Hispanic candidates from the Democratic Party to come forward and the immediate future seems more profitable for that party.

Furthermore, as a result of monumental voter registration efforts on the part of the Democrats, they now outnumber Republicans in the state by some 600,000 registered voters, with over 2 million independent or third party registrants. Nevertheless, after the election the state remained moderate to conservative in political ideology, with 39% conservatives, 37% moderates and 20% liberals, (Gallup Poll. 2009) an ideological distribution that is likely to benefit Republican candidates.

Despite the forces that potentially favor the Democrats, in the absence of reapportionment, the only real prospects for change in the outcomes of the races for the U.S. Congress lie in the normal off-year dynamics of elections in the U.S. Some candidates will be affected by drop off in turnout and by the standing of the President in public opinion polls. As was the case in 2008, others will be affected by their own personal behavior and by their stance on specific policy issues or events. As this is being written, a strong anti-incumbent sentiment is sweeping both Florida and the nation and may have implications for specific districts. Congressional campaigns likely to be affected by one or several of the factors mentioned above are those in districts 24, 2, 8, 12 and 6.

STATE LEGISLATIVE ELECTIONS

The primary factors that affected the outcome of the state legislative races in 2008 were apportionment, incumbency, and term limits. While the apportionment scheme in place in 2008 will still be in effect in the 2010 elections, changes in the other two variables create the possibility for minor changes in the partisan distribution of seats in the new state legislature. Nevertheless, the Republicans appear poised to retain comfortable control in both legislative bodies.

In the State Senate, 23 seats will be up for election and over half (13) will be open seats. Six of these are the result of term limits, but seven came open as a result of efforts on the part of incumbents to run for other offices in the state. Of the 13 open seats, eight are currently held by Republicans and five by Democrats. Our measure of "generic competitiveness" suggests that five of these seats are likely to be "tight" races and 5 others will be "competitive." When other dynamics are factored in, we expect four seats will be "tight," that is decided by 5% or less.

Among these districts are numbers 14 and 16 which were two of the seats that flipped in 2006 and could very well flip back and realign with the voter registration and performance of the respective districts. The third battleground seat is Senate 25. This District is currently occupied by a Republican who is running for higher office. The open seat here has a performance advantage of R+ 2.5% contrasted with a registration advantage of D+6.15%. The fourth battleground is Senate District 27, which has a registration advantage of D+4.3% and a performance advantage of D+7.78%. The final outcome is likely to be a draw, with each party gaining one seat.

In the Florida House in 2010, there will be 24 districts with term limited members; 21 are currently held by Republicans and 3 by Democrats. Over half of these seats (15) are identified as potentially tight (9) or competitive (6) when measured by the district performance criteria. Using this same criterion, we suggest that another 26 non term limited House seats are also likely to be either tight or competitive. Thus, in 2010, candidates in 47 state House seats are potentially facing competitive elections, using the generic measure of competitiveness. Nevertheless, once the influence of apportionment, incumbency and term limits are factored in, competition is likely to decline and only 35 will be truly competitive. We predict that the major political parties will divide these elections relatively evenly with either netting a one seat pick up. This outcome would leave the Republicans in control of the House with 75 to 77 seats.

LEGISLATIVE REAPPORTIONMENT

The apportionment system put into place in 2002 has had a substantial effect on the partisan distribution of elected officials in both the Florida congressional delegation and in the Florida State Legislature and objective observers of electoral politics in the state concede that the plan has weighted the odds in favor of the Republican Party. In a state where Democrats outnumber Republicans by over 600,000 registrants, the Republicans control the congressional delegation and both houses of the state legislature by sizeable numbers.

Since 2002, Democrats, along with a handful of Republicans, have criticized the process that created this plan and have fought to remediate it through a constitutional amendment that would remove or limit the legislature's control over the process. In 2010 a group of activists using the name FairDistrictsFlorida successfully collected over a million (1,650,000) signatures asking that such an amendment be placed on the ballot in 2010. Two amendments, one for Congress and another for the state legislature, were approved and both will voted on in November. Each will prohibit drawing district lines to favor or disfavor any incumbent or political party and require that district lines be compact and utilize existing political and geographical boundaries.

In the aftermath of this success, Republicans in the legislature, along with two African American Democrats in the State Senate and one in the House, also passed an amendment regarding redistricting procedures. This amendment, which some opponents referred to as a "silver bullet", kept the requirements regarding incumbency, compactness and contiguity, but incorporated a statement permitting legislators to use "community of common interest" as a criterion. Proponents of this amendment argued that it would allow the legislature to continue to adhere to the Federal Voting Rights Act which required that minorities be provided an opportunity to elect candidates of their choice and to group areas with large numbers of minorities together in order to give them better representation. Opponents, remembering the partisan effect of such groupings in 2002, claimed it was a way for Republicans to preserve their numbers in both Congress and the state legislature, and challenged the amendment in state court. On July 8, a circuit judge struck it down because it was too confusing for voters to understand. The outcome of the appeal to this ruling and the vote on these amendments—which need 60% of those who vote in the 2010 election—will have a significant effect on Florida politics in the next decade.

Bibliography

Ash, Arlene and John Lampeti. 2008. "Florida 2006: Can Statistics Tell Us Who Won Congressional District 13?" *Chance* (Springer) 21 (2) Spring. 18–24.

Balz, Dan and Haynes Johnson, 2009. *The Battle for America, 2008.* New York: Viking.

Barone, Michael and Richard Cohen. 2004. *Almanac of American Politics.* Washington, D.C.: National Journal Group.

Bender, Michael. 2008. "430,000 New Voters Registered in Florida." *PalmBeachPost.com.* October 4. Found at www.palmbeachpost.com/state/content/state/epaper/2008/10/1004_newvoters.html.

Bridges, Tyler. 2002. "GOP's Strategy Flips Florida Politics: Redistricting Plan Hurt Democrats." *Miami Herald.* December 1.

Caeser, James W., Andrew Busch and John J. Pitney, Jr. 2009. *Epic Journey.* Lanham, Md.: Rowman and Littlefield.

Campbell, Angus, Philip Converse, Warren Miller and Donald E. Stokes. 1961. *The American Voter.*

Carson, Jamie L., Erik Engstrom and Jason Roberts. 2007. "Candidate Quality, the Personal Vote and the Incumbency Advantage in Congress." *American Political Science Review.* Vol 101 (No 2) May. 289–301.

Chalian, David. 2010. "Rudy Giuliani Backs Marco Rubio Over Charlie Crist." Blogs. abcnews.com/the note/2010/04/rudy-giuliani-backs-marco-rubio-over-charlie-c. 6/25/2010.

Crew, Robert, Slater Bayliss and Monica Moore. 2010. "Explaining the Outcome of the 2008 Elections in Florida." A paper presented at the 17th Biannual Citadel Symposium on Southern Politics. Charleston, S.C.: March 4–5, 2010.

Crotty, William. 2009. "The Bush Presidency and the 2008 Presidential Election." William Crotty, *Winning the Presidency 2008.* Boulder: Paradigm Publishers.

Deslatte, Aaron and Jim Stratton. 2008. "Will Obama's Win Have A Lasting Effect on Politics?"OrlandoSentinel.org. November 6. Found at orlandosentinel.com/news_politics/2008/11/will_obamas_win.html.

Gallup Poll. 2009. *State of the States*. "Political Ideology." August.

Haque, Umair. 2008. "Obama's Seven Lessons for Radical Innovators." Blogs.harvard business.org/haque/2008/11/obamas_seven_lessons_for_radic.html.

Harfoush, Rahaf. 2009. *Yes We Did*. Berkeley, Calif.: New Riders.

Holmes, Elizabeth and Elizabeth Williamson. 2008. "McCain Team Hustles Amid Rising Interest." *Wall Street Journal*. Sept. 15.

Institute of Politics, Kennedy School of Government. 2009. *Campaign for President*.

Junn, Lee, Wong, Ramakrishnan, "National Asian American Survey." 2009.

Klas, Mary Ellen. 2008. "Inside Story: How Obama Won Florida." *The Miami Herald*. November 8.

Levitt, Ron. 2008 "Democratic Efforts: Celebrity and Grassroots, Paying Off in Florida." Huffingtonpost.com/ron_levitt/fla-celebrity-party-and-g. July 30.

Lichtman, Alan. 2002. "Report on State House and State Senate Districts in Florida." A Report prepared for petitioners in Florida Supreme Court case SC02-194.

Lizza, Ryan. 2008. "Battle Plans. How Obama Won." *The New Yorker*. November 17.

Maisel, Sandy, Walter Stone and Cherie Maestas. 2000. "Quality Challengers to Congressional Incumbents, Can Better Candidates Be Found?" in Paul Hernson, *Playing Hardball: Campaigning for the US Congress*. New York: Prentice Hall.

Mark, David. 2006. *Going Dirty*. Lanham, Md.: Rowman and Littlefield.

Martin, Jonathan. 2008. "McCain Pushes to Raise Coin, Build Org in Fl." politico.com/blogs/jonathanmartin/0108.

Martinez, Michael. 2009. "Battleground Voters: Partisanship, Issues and Retrospective Evaluations in Florida, 2008." *Florida Focus*. BEBR, University of Florida. May.

MacGillis, Alec and Alice Crites. 2008. "Registration Gains Favor Democrats," *Washington Post*. October 6.

MacGillis, Alec. 2008. "Democrats Predominate Among Newly Registered Florida Voters," *Washington Post*. October 7. Found at http://voices.washingtonpost.com/44/2008/10/07.

McDonald, Michael and Samuel Popkin. 2001. "The Myth of the Vanishing Voter." *American Political Science Review*. 95 (4): 963–974.

Moreno, Dario and Nicol Rae, "Ethnicity and Partisanship: The Case of the 18th Congressional District in Miami." www.fiu.edu/~morenod/scholar/illeana.htm.

MSNBC. 2008. Florida Presidential Exit Poll. www.msnbc.msn.com/id/25383667/.

Newsweek. 2008. "How He did It: Going Into Battle." (www.newswweek.com/id/167865/output/print).

Opperman, Patrick. 2008. "Great Schlep Pitches Obama to Florida Jews." www.cnn.com/2008/POLITICS/10/13/great.schlep/index.html).

Padgett, Tim. 2008. "What's Got McCain Down in Florida?" www.time.com/time/printout/0,8816,1851940,00.html.

"Panic at the Pasco." 2008. *The Reid Report*. Blog.reidreport.com/2008/10/panic-at-pasco.html.

Republican Party of Florida. "RPOF Launches Statewide Voter Initiative." 2009. RPOF Press Release. June 2.

Reynolds, Gretchen. 1993. "Voter of Confidence," *Chicago Magazine*. January.

Sharockman, Aaron. 2007. "McCain's Florida Hopes Fade," *St Petersburg Times.* July 4.

Sizemore, Justin. 2008. "The Democratic Ground Game." August 14. www.centerforpolitics.org/crystalball/article.php?id=JMS2008081401.

Smith, Adam. 2008. "McCain, Obama Florida Machines Get Cranking." *St Petersburg Times.* August 10.

Stone. Doug, 2008. "With Obama's Message Clear, GOP Worries About McCain's Shifting Slogans." *MinnPost.com.* June 25. Found at www.minnpost.com/stories/2008/06/25/2362/.

Stratton, Jim 2008. "Obama's Florida Payroll Grows Again."*OrlandoSentinel.com* . August 11.

Stratton, Jim. 2008 "Some GOP Insiders say McCain has Botched Campaign to Win Florida." *OrlandoSentinel.com.* October 19.

Todd, Chuck and Sheldon Gawiser, *How Barack Obama Won.* 2009. New York; Vintage Books.

Wagner, Kevin and Eric Prior. 2008. "The Legislature and the Legislative Process in Florida." In J. Edwin Benton, ed. *Government and Politics in Florida.* Gainesville, Fl.: University Press of Florida.

Index

Abramoff, Jack, 92
absentee and early voting, 28–32
ACORN, 47
advertising, political: McCain campaign, 25–26; Obama campaign, 21–22; Republican primary, 8, 9
African Americans: apportionment/reapportionment process and, 112; District 3 congressional races, 79; District 23 congressional races, 92; Obama support, 57, 58; in Orange County, 35; party identification, 40, 50; voter registration, 50, 51
Alachua County, 34
Allen, Bob, 120
The American Voter (Campbell, Converse, Miller, and Stokes), 4
apportionment/reapportionment, 112–15, 127–28
Asian Americans, 40
Associated Press: early and absentee voting analysis, 29; Florida general election projection, 27
Ausley, Lorrane, 119
Axelrod, David, 18

baby boomers, 60–61, 65
Bense, Alan, 9
Benson, Holly, 118
Benson, Laura, 121–22
Biden, Joe, 6, 12
Bilirakis, Gus Michael, 83
Bilirakis, Michael, 83
Blythe, Steve, 87
Boulware, Peter, 119
Bowen, Marty, 120
Boyd, Alan, 79–80
Boyd, Debbie, 119
Bradenton, 86
Bradshaw, Sally, 9, 35
Brevard County: District 24 congressional races, 92; Hispanic population, 40; state legislative races, 120
Broward County: Democratic Party support, 20, 34, 47; District 20 congressional races, 90; District 21 congressional races, 90; District 22 congressional races, 91; Jewish Community Leadership Committee, 19
Brown, Corrine, 79–80
Brownback, Sam, 6
Brown-Waite, Ginny, 81
Buchanan, Vern, 85–86
Bush, George W.: policy issues, 69; presidential job performance, 69–70.

See also presidential election (2000); presidential election (2004)
Bush, Jeb, 9, 26

Campaign for Change (CFC), 18–19
campaign fundraising and spending: in congressional races, 96; Democratic primary, 12; Republican primary, 9, 10; in state legislative races, 113
campaign organization structure, 20, 24
candidate background and experience, 70–72, 96–99
Cape Coral, 86
Cardenas, Al, 9
Carter, Jimmy, 34
Castor, Kathy, 84
CFC (Campaign for Change), 18–19
change, campaign message of, 71
Chapin, Linda, 82
Cheney, Dick, 6
Christian, Todd, 120
Clarke, Donna, 121
Clay County, 119–20
Clinton, Bill, 34
Clinton, Hillary: campaign fundraising, 12; candidacy announcement, 6; Florida primary performance, 12–13; Iowa caucus, 12; Nevada caucus, 12; New Hampshire primary, 12; poll performance, 11
college graduates, 61
Collier County: District 25 congressional races, 93; primary results, 11; voter registration allegiance, 50
congressional races, 78–93; apportionment/reapportionment impact, 127–28; District 1, 78–79; District 2, 79–80; District 3, 79–80; District 4, 80; District 5, 80–81; District 6, 81; District 7, 81–82; District 8, 82–83, 125; District 9, 83; District 10, 83–84; District 11, 84; District 12, 84; District 13, 84–86; District 14, 86–87; District 15, 87; District 16, 87–88; District 17, 88–89; District 18, 89, 125; District 19, 89; District 20, 90; District 21, 90–91, 125; District 22, 91; District 23, 92; District 24, 92–93; District 25, 93; incumbency success, 94–105; introduction, 75–78; summary, 106
conservatives: Huckabee support, 9–10; impact of, 14–15; McCain support, 60
Cook Partisan Voting Index, 77–78
Cox, John H., 6
Cramer, William, 83
Crenshaw, Ander, 80
Crisafulli, Steve, 120
Crist, Charlie: early voting, 29; McCain endorsement, 9
Cuban Americans: apportionment/reapportionment process and, 113; District 21 congressional races, 90–91; District 25 congressional races, 93; political impact of, 40; Republican Party support, 50–51. *See also* Hispanics
Curtis, Clint, 92

Davis, Jim, 84
Daytona Beach, 82
Delegates, 5, 7
Democracia USA, 51
Democratic National Committee (DNC): Florida Campaign for Change, 18–19; Florida primary controversy, 7, 13–14
Democratic Party: African American supporters, 57; campaign strategies, 17–23; congressional elections, 75, 77, 106; delegates, 13; early and absentee voting, 29–32; election results, 32–34; Hispanic supporters, 57; history in Florida, 4, 47–50; presidential candidates, 6–7; primaries, 11–13; state legislative

races, 109–12; voter registration, 44, 46–47; voter turnout, 55
Democrats, Obama support, 57
demographic changes, 125
DeSoto County, 51
Diaz-Balart, Lincoln, 90–91
Diaz-Balart, Mario, 93–94
DiTerlizzi, Michael, 121
DNC. *See* Democratic National Committee (DNC)
Dodd, Chris, 6, 12
Domino, Carl, 121
Duval County: District 6 congressional races, 81; Obama campaign, 18; presidential election results, 32; Republican primary results, 11

early and absentee voting, 28–32
economy, 66–69
educational attainment, and voting patterns, 57, 62
Edwards, John: campaign fundraising, 12; candidacy announcement, 6; Florida primary performance, 12; Iowa caucus, 12; New Hampshire primary, 12; poll performance, 12; South Carolina primary, 12
Eisnaugle, Eric, 120
elections. *See* congressional races; presidential election (2008); state legislative races
energy, 67

FairDistrictsFlorida, 128
family income, and voting patterns, 57, 62
FDP (Florida Democratic Party), 5, 11–13
Feeney, Tom, 92–93
Fetterman, Adam, 121
Fitzgerald, Peter, 121
Flagler County: 2008 vs. 2004 election outcomes, 28; Obama support, 34; party allegiance, 50
Florida: election delegates, 5, 7; electoral votes, 5
Florida Democratic Party (FDP), 5, 11–13
Florida Women for Obama, 19
Foley, Mark, 87–88
Ford, Clay, 118
Ford, Rick, 121
FOX News polls, 9
future election factors, 125–28

Gadsen County, 34, 79
Gallup Daily poll, 27
Garcia, Joe, 93
Gardner, Andy, 120
gays and lesbians, 90
gender gap, 60
Gilchrist County, 119
Gilmore, Jim, 6
Giuliani, Rudy: campaign strategy, 7–8, 9; candidacy announcement, 6; Florida primary performance, 10–11; Florida primary strategy, 8; Iowa caucus performance, 8; McCain endorsement, 11; New Hampshire primary performance, 8; poll performance, 10
Gore, Al, 44. *See also* presidential election (2000)
Goss, Porter, 86
Gravel, Mike, 6
Grayson, Alan, 83
Green Party, 116
ground campaigns: McCain, 23–25; Obama, 17–21
group voting, 56–65; in 2004 vs. 2008, 56–60; in Florida vs. nation, 62–65; introduction, 56
Gulf Breeze, 118
Gulf County, 55

Hagenmaier, Bob, 120
Haitian Americans, 92
Hardee County, 51

Harrell, Gayle, 121
Harris, Katherine, 85
Hastings, Alcee, 92
Healthcare, 66
Hendry County, 47
Hernando County, 50
Highlands County, 55
Hillsborough County: 2008 vs. 2004 election outcomes, 50; District 9 congressional races, 83; District 12 congressional races, 84; Obama campaign, 18, 21; voter registration allegiance, 50
Hispanics: apportionment/reapportionment process and, 113; District 8 congressional races, 82; District 21 congressional races, 90; District 25 congressional races, 93; future election impact, 125–26; McCain support, 11, 60; Obama support, 57, 60, 62; party allegiance, 51; political impact, 36, 40; voter registration, 50–51; voting patterns (2004 vs. 2008), 65. *See also* Cuban Americans
Hood, Glenda, 9
House of Representatives (Florida), elections. *See* state legislative races
House of Representatives (U.S.), elections. *See* congressional races
Huckabee, Mike: campaign strategy, 9; candidacy announcement, 6; Florida primary performance, 9–11; Florida primary strategy, 8; Iowa caucus, 7; New Hampshire primary, 8; poll performance, 7, 8; South Carolina primary, 8
Hunter, Duncan, 6

incumbency success: in congressional races, 94–105; in state legislative races, 111, 113–14
Independents: African American supporters, 50; Hispanic supporters, 51; Obama support, 57; voter registration, 50, 51; vote share increase (2004 vs. 2008), 61
Iowa caucus, 7, 10
Iraq War, 66, 67
Ireland, Andy, 85

Jacksonville: District 3 congressional races, 80; District 4 congressional races, 80; early voting results, 32
Jacobson v. Martin, 117
Jefferson County: Democratic Party support, 34; District 2 congressional races, 79; state legislative races, 118
Jennings, Christine, 85–86
Jennings, Toni, 9
Jewish Americans: District 18 congressional races, 89; District 19 congressional races, 89; Obama campaign, 19
Jewish Community Leadership Committees, 19
Justice, Charlie, 111

Keller, Ric, 82–83
Kerry, John. *See* presidential election (2004)
Keyes, Alan, 6
Klein, Ron, 78
Kosmas, Suzanne, 91, 92
Kucinich, Dennis, 6

Lafayette County, 119
Lake County: Hispanics in, 40; state legislative race, 119; voter registration allegiance, 50; voter turnout, 55
Leon County: Democratic Party support, 16, 34, 79; state legislative races, 118; voter turnout, 51
liberals, 57
Lichtman, Alan, 113

Mack, Connie, IV, 86–87
Mahoney, Tim, 88
Manatee County, 121

Marion County, 82, 119
Martin County, 121
Martinez, Mel, 9, 85
Martin; Jacobson v., 117
McCain, John: campaign message, 16, 17, 71; candidacy announcement, 6; election results, 27–28; Florida primary performance, 11; Florida primary strategy, 9–10, 23; Giuliani's endorsement, 11; ground campaign, 23–25; group voting patterns, 56–65; Iowa caucus, 7; New Hampshire primary, 8, 9; Obama campaign's TV ad attacks, 22; policy issues, 66–69; poll performance, 7, 10, 27; South Carolina primary, 8, 10; TV and radio ads, 25–26, 71; voter registration efforts, 47; voters' association with Bush, 69–70
McCollum, Bill, 82
media. *See* television and radio
Meek, Carrie, 88
Meek, Kendrick, 88
men, voting patterns of, 60
Merritt Island, 87
Miami, 88–89
Miami-Dade County: Democratic Party support, 16, 20, 34; District 20 congressional races, 90; District 21 congressional races, 90; District 25 congressional races, 99; early and absentee voting, 32; Jewish Community Leadership Committee, 30; Republican primary results, 11; voter registration allegiance, 50
Mica, John, 82
Michigan primaries, 8
Miller, Brian, 121
Miller, Daniel, 85
Miller, Jeff, 78
minor party candidates, in state legislative races, 116–17
Monroe County, 34, 93
MSMBC polls, 21, 25
Myers, Linda, 119
Naples, 86
Nashua County, 80
National Republican Trust PAC, 40
negative ads, 21–22, 25–26, 71
Negron, Joe, 87–88
Nehr, Peter, 120
Nevada caucus, 12
New Hampshire primary, 8, 12
new voters, 60, 62

Obama, Barack: campaign fundraising, 18–19; campaign message, 16–17, 71; campaign organization structure, 17–19; candidacy announcement, 6; congressional race impact, 106; election results, 27, 34–35, 40; Florida primary performance, 13; Florida primary strategy, 12–13; ground campaign, 17–21; group voting patterns, 56–61; Iowa caucus, 12; McCain campaign's TV ad attacks, 25–26; Nevada caucus, 12; New Hampshire primary, 12; personal qualities, 70–72; policy issues, 66–69; poll performance, 12, 27; race as factor in election, 70; South Carolina primary, 12; TV and radio ads, 21–23, 71; voter registration efforts, 46–47; Winfrey's endorsement, 12
Obama for America, 17–18
Oelrich, Steve, 111
Orange County: congressional elections, 82–83; Democratic Party gains, 35; District 8 congressional races, 82; District 24 congressional races, 92; Hispanics in, 40; Republican primary results, 11; state legislative races, 120, 122; voter registration allegiance, 50
Orlando: District 3 congressional races, 79; District 8 congressional races, 82; Jewish Community Leadership Committee, 19; state legislative races, 120

Ormond Beach, 82
Ortiz, Belinda, 122
Osceola County: 2008 vs. 2004 election outcomes, 34–35; Democratic Party gains, 35; District 12 congressional races, 84; Hispanics in, 40; state legislative races, 122

Palm Beach County: Democratic Party support, 18, 34; District 22 congressional races, 91; Jewish Community Leadership Committee, 19; state legislative races, 121; voter registration allegiance, 50
party competition, 34–36
Pasco County, 24, 83
Paul, Ron, 6
Pensacola, 118
Pickens, Joe, 119
Pinellas County: 2008 vs. 2004 election outcomes, 34; Democratic Party support, 34; District 9 congressional races, 83; District 10 congressional races, 83; Obama campaign, 21; party allegiance, 50; state legislative races, 120
Plouffe, David, 13
policy issues, 66–69
political advertising. *See under* television and radio
Polk County: District 12 congressional races, 84; Hispanics in, 40; state legislative races, 120
Porter, Elizabeth, 119
Posey, Bill, 87
presidential election (2000): gender gap, 60; margin of victory, 44; voter registration and turnout, 44, 45
presidential election (2004): county voting results vs. 2008, 34–36, 55; early and absentee voting, 28–32; group voting, 56–65; Osceola County results, 28
presidential election (2008): campaign strategies, 15–26; Democrats, 16, 17–23; Overview, 16–17; Republicans, 16, 23–26; Overview, 3–4; Results, 27–40; county-by-county results, 34–36; early and absentee voting, 28–31; media projections, 27; party competitiveness, 36–40; patterns, 32–34; polls, 27; strategic context, 15. *See also* primaries; voting behavior
presidential job performance, 69–70
primaries: Florida, 5–14; closed primary structure, 116–17; Democrats, 11–13; Introduction, 5; Republicans, 7–11; Summary, 13–14; timing dispute between DNC and Florida Democratic Party, 5, 13; Iowa caucus, 7, 12; Michigan, 8; Nevada caucus, 12; New Hampshire, 8, 12; South Carolina, 8–9, 12
Prior, Eric, 110
Project Vote, 47
public opinion polls: Democratic primary, 11–12; presidential election, 27; Republican primary, 7, 9, 10
Puerto Rican Americans, 35
Putnam, Adam, 84
Putnam County, 119

race, as factor in election, 70
radio. *See* television and radio
Rasmussen Poll, 27
Redistricting, 110, 112–13, 114, 127–28
religious affiliation, and voting patterns, 57, 62
religious right, 9
Republican Jewish Coalition, 26
Republican National Committee (RNC), 26
Republican Party: African American supporters, 50; campaign strategies, 16, 17, 23–26; congressional elections, 77–78, 106; delegates, 5; early and absentee voting, 29–31; election results, 27–28; Hispanic

supporters, 50; history in Florida, 4, 34–36; presidential candidates, 6; primaries, 7–11; state legislative races, 109–22; voter registration, 44, 47; voter turnout, 55
Republican Party of Florida (RFOP), 24–25
Republicans: McCain support, 57; Obama support, 61
RFOP (Republican Party of Florida), 24–25
Richardson, Bill: candidacy announcement, 6; Iowa caucus, 12; New Hampshire primary, 12
Richman, Gerald, 89
Rivera, David, 10
RNC (Republican National Committee), 25
Romney, Mitt: candidacy announcement, 6; Florida primary performance, 8–9; Iowa caucus, 7; Michigan primary, 8; New Hampshire primary, 8; poll performance, 7, 10; South Carolina primary, 8
Rooney, Tom, 88
Ros-Lehtinen, Ileana, 89
Rove, Karl, 24
Rubio, Marco, 10

Sarasota, 19, 121
Sarasota County, 84
Sasso, Tony, 115, 120
Scarborough, Joe, 78
Schale, Steve, 17, 47, 111
Schneider, Jan, 85, 86
Seminole County, 40, 92
Senate (Florida), elections. *See* state legislative races
Senate (U.S.), elections. *See* congressional races
Shaw, Clay, 91
Silverman, Sarah, 19
Sink, Alex, 119, 120
Siplin, Gary, 122
Slade, Tom, 23
social group voting. *See* group voting
South Carolina primary, 8, 12
Stanzel, Dwight, 119
state legislative races, 109–22; apportionment/reapportionment impact, 112–13, 114, 127–28; future factors, 127–28; incumbency success, 113, 115; introduction, 109–11; minor party candidates, 116–17; outcomes, 111–12; term limits, 114, 115–16; tight races, 17–122
St. Augustine, 82
Stearns, Cliff, 81
St. Johns County, 51
St. Lucie County, 34, 121
St. Petersburg, 83
Sumter County, 55, 80
Suwannee County, 119

Tallahasse, 118
Tampa, 31, 84
Tampa Bay area: independent voters, 16; Jewish Community Leadership Committee, 19; McCain support, 11
Tancredo, Tom, 6
television and radio: advertising: McCain campaign, 25–26; Obama campaign, 21–22; Republican primary, 8, 9; election coverage, 27
term limits, 112, 114
terrorism, 67, 68
Thompson, Fred, 6, 8
Thompson, Tommy: candidacy announcement, 6; Iowa caucus, 7; South Carolina primary, 8
Thrasher, John, 9
Thurman, Karen, 81
TNS Media Intelligence, 21, 25

Van Zant, Steve, 119
VAP (voting age population), 43, 44, 51
Vasilinda, Michelle Rehwinkle, 119
VEP (voter eligible population), 43, 44, 51

Vero Beach, 87
Villages, 81
Vilsack, Tom, 6
Volusia County: Democratic Party support, 34; District 24 congressional races, 92; Hispanics in, 40; state legislative races, 19
VoteBuilder, 20
voter attitudes, 66–72; candidate qualities, 70–72; experience vs. change campaign message, 71; negative ads, 71–72; policy issues, 66–69; presidential job performance, 69–70
voter eligible population (VEP), 43, 44, 51
voter identification and contact, 18, 20–22
voter registration: congressional district analysis, 77–78; Democratic vs. Republican Party efforts, 46–51; in Florida vs. nation, 44
voter turnout: baby boomers, 57; by county, 51–55; Democratic vs. Republican Party, 55; in Florida vs. nation, 44; measurement of, 51; youth, 61
voting age population (VAP), 43, 44, 51
voting behavior: group voting, 56–65; introduction, 56; policy issues, 66–69; voter attitudes, 66–72. *See also* voter registration; voter turnout
voting machine failures, 85–86

Wagner, Kevin, 110
Wallach, Ari, 19
Washington Post: on Tom Feeney, 92
Wasserman-Schultz, Debbie, 90
Watson, Terry, 18
web sites, of Obama campaign, 20
Webster, Daniel, 10
Weldon, Dave, 87
West, Allen, 91
Wexler, Robert, 90
white voters, 57
Wilton Manors, 90
Winfrey, Oprah, 12
women: Florida Women for Obama, 19; voting patterns of, 60
Wood, John, 120
Wright, Jeremiah, 26
write-in candidates, in state legislative races, 116

Young, Bill, 83
Youth, 61

www.ingramcontent.com/pod-product-compliance
Lightning Source LLC
Chambersburg PA
CBHW050522280326
41932CB00014B/2416

* 9 7 8 0 7 6 1 8 5 4 2 6 5 *